Appreciations for "My Journey of Hope"

Powerful. Thoughtful. Honest. Scary. Without guile. And…right. Amazingly, unpretentiously right.

Bookstores and blogs are filled with words about death experiences and loss. The grief. The regret. The pain. It's all there.

What's almost entirely missing, however, are the details. Honest, real-life details. The normal, everyday events that thread their way through these emotions, and live on in our hearts, minds, and souls.

Don's book, thankfully, is filled with the real life that surrounds a journey with the one you love. One who is heading for, or has gone, to the other side. The emotions are all there, to be sure.

But the Real Story never gets lost. Through Don's daily journey – his interactions with family, friends, and (most especially) himself and God – we learn. And we do that because Don learns.

Dr. Stan Gaede

> *President, Christian College Consortium*
> *Scholar-in-Residence, Gordon College*
> *Author of "An Incomplete Guide to the Rest of Your Life"*
> *and "Surprised by God"*

I hope I never walk the pathway that Don has traveled, but on life's journey we all encounter obstacles of pain, sorrow, loss and disappointment. Don has mapped the course well for us.

He recounts not only the pathway to hope but annotates his emotions and insights each step along the way. Read it now, before the pain of loss clouds your perspective. Reread it when the troubles of life seem to paralyze your personal journey to hope.

Dr. Dan Bolin

> *International Director, Christian Camping International*
> *Author of "How to be Your Wife's Best Friend" and*
> *"How to be Your Daughter's Daddy"*

My Journey to Hope
Don Goehner
Copyright 2010

ISBN 978-0-9831285-0-2

For permission to reprint or quote material from this book, contact:
Don Goehner
3566 Sunnyvale Court
San Jose, CA 95117
info@goehnergroup.com
408-202-2948

Cover: The design reflects the comfort and truth of a Scripture that sustained me throughout my journey, a verse I came to cherish, *"The path of the righteous is the first gleam of dawn, shining ever brighter till the full light of day."*
Prov. 4:18

Design by Kathy Skye,
SkyeDesign Interactive
www.skyedesign.biz

Dedication

*To Terri, Todd and Trina, whose mother was
the love of my life and who loved them
unconditionally from the moment of their
birth to the moment of her death.*

Don Goehner is president of The Goehner Group, the company he founded in 1982 to assist ministry organizations in achieving their mission, vision and goals through stewardship, marketing, and leadership consultation. Don graduated with a degree in sociology from Westmont College and a master's degree in business administration from Pepperdine University. He's directed several ministry organizations; been a college administrator, faculty member, and development officer; was national chairman of the Young Life Capernaum Committee for four years and has served as a Westmont trustee since 1986.

Contents

Part One: *Ten Months and Ten Days*

Celebrating Bev Goehner's final year	15
Serving God and people as a couple	16
Connecting with friends and family	22
Final visits, vacations and reunions	33
Darkening days	41
Making the most of the time	45
"Dad, we are losing Mom."	50
Our God is faithful	57
Honoring Bev Goehner	62

Part Two: *The Next Chapter in my Journey*

Reflection and celebration	71
Journal to Bev	87
Second journal to Bev	93
New Years' reflections	100
Learning to walk in - and through - grief	107
My dad, my companion in grief	117
Eighteen months that changed my life	119
Special times for grandpa and grandsons	127
Living the new normal	130
Coming to faith, growing in God	136
New beginnings	139

Appendix

My letter to Bev	148
Anniversary letter to Bev	157
Letters to my children	162
"It's been three years"	165
Grief-recovery workshop presentation	169
My mom's graduation	178
Messages from our prayer team	180
Messages to our prayer team	184
Books on grieving	205

FORWARD

Dr. Gayle D. Beebe, President
Westmont College

I first met Don Goehner in the late 1980s in Roger Minthorne's kitchen. Don was in Portland Ore., to help with Twin Rocks Friends Camp and Roger was the head elder of the church where I was pastor. Even then, Don struck me as someone I could trust. He had an ease and honesty, combined with grace, I found refreshing.

Today, Don and I serve together at Westmont College; he as a member of our board of trustees and me as president. Because of my wife's longtime interest in grief-recovery ministry we have had numerous conversations about his wife, Bev. Although Bev is the main character in this book, the primary issue is the goodness of God - even when we grieve.

This book is a testimony to Don's determination to grieve hard and heal fully. He has walked the lonely road of decline and death, and learned lessons few ever master and most try hard to avoid. It is a book filled with mileposts that mark the way-stations we will all find, if God has us walk this path. More than anything, this book is a gentle and grace-filled reminder that God is sufficient if we learn to trust Him.

To know Don is to experience a frankness and confidence in Christ I rarely encounter. Don prays and then trusts God for the results. There are times when I think Don underestimates how hard it is for many Christians to take God at His word. But even after Don prays and his prayers remain unanswered, he doesn't turn away, but prays even more intently, trusting God for even deeper answers.

Ultimately, this book is an invitation to understand and embrace the cycle of grief we inevitably face, either as victims or as companions. Eventually, we all suffer and it is in our suffering that we choose our attitude and learn to affirm the goodness of God, even when it is difficult.

I'm grateful Don wrote this book and especially thankful for those who have entered his grief and loss to help and encourage him along the way. Caryl Taylor, who became Don's wife, is especially courageous and evokes our admiration and praise. She has entered his journey as a sign of God's hope and promise in the midst of suffering.

Don, thanks for leaning into the pain so we could all learn to negotiate this path better.

INTRODUCTION

This was never intended to be a book.

Initially, I wrote to help relieve my grief and capture the myriad of feelings I was experiencing. I thought I would give a copy to each of my children, my son-in-law and my grandsons. After my initial week of writing (during the summer of 2007 on the Sunshine Coast of British Columbia), I realized this might become something people would want to read. Trusted colleagues and close friends confirmed my decision and urged me to make my story available to others.

I continued to write while on my personal retreats and during business trips. I wrote journals and continued to think and reflect on the 48 years I was married to Bev Knowles Goehner, and how that relationship and this woman shaped my life. At the same time, I worked hard at – and wrote about – grieving. I was determined not to get stuck in my pain and loss, while becoming spiritually and emotionally healthy.

One day, I realized my original idea - to write about Bev's final year (2006) - was only part of the story. I needed to write about the hard work of grieving and what I learned during that period of my life. The past four years have been among the hardest I have experienced, yet I wouldn't trade them for any other four years. I have been in pain; been stretched; and felt loneliness, joy, gratefulness, and wonder at what God has done in my life during this experience.

What you will read is at times raw and painful, humorous, and profoundly sad. But I trust you will discover one golden thread throughout the book – God's faithfulness. In the more-than 50 years I have been a Christian I have often spoken of God's faithfulness and sufficiency – but primarily as an observer of his work in the lives of others. Today, however, I understand his faithfulness and sufficiency as one who has experienced them daily.

There are so many people to thank, people whose presence changed me during this journey. Without their specific encouragements and challenges, I would have stumbled more often than I did. Within minutes of Bev's death on November 10, 2006, I was surrounded by friends and pastors who ministered to me. Many continue to do so today.

In naming several key participants in my journey to hope, I fear I may leave someone out. If I do, please forgive my oversight and know I am grateful for every one of you.

- Keith Potter, former senior pastor of Saratoga Federated Church (SFC), and his wife, Sue, have been with me throughout, but especially so during my first Thanksgiving alone (less than two weeks after Bev's death).
- Kevin Friesen, who was on the pastoral staff of SFC at the time, spent the first 36 hours following Bev's death at my side, and helped me begin the grief process.
- Nancy Jensen, a longtime friend and widow, was extremely helpful in the first few weeks and months. Her motto, You can't choose your circumstances but you can choose your attitude, is forever burned into my psyche.
- Ed McDowell, a client of The Goehner Group but more importantly, a special friend, was immediately available for conversation. His encouragement has been so helpful.

- Linda Connors, my assistant at the time, who became a confidant and "my younger sister" without whom I could not have gotten through the memorial service and the first week of being a widower.
- Sue Cairns and I began as acquaintances but became friends as we grieved the loss of our spouses. She has been a prayer partner and true soul mate in the grief journey.
- Tom and Viv Nelson, a couple with whom Bev and I vacationed. Tom's challenge to me, which you will read about, was a turning point in my recovery. Viv helped teach me to how to cook and constantly checked in and prayed.
- Steve Van Atta, my editor, who has helped me to write articles for more than 20 years. He has the ability to make it appear that I can actually write.

There are numerous others: Larry Ballenger, a 50-year friend; Gary Low, my business mentor; Fred Miller, business manager of The Goehner Group; Wes and Jene Jeske, Bev's sister and brother-in-law; Dr. Gayle Beebe, president of Westmont College, and his wife, Pam; the entire Westmont Trustee Board…to name but a few.

Finally, I'm so grateful to my family for the special part they had in this story:

- My sisters Elvera and Eldora, both widows who had walked this path before me.
- My daughters Trina and Terri, who were supportive while they processed their own grief. Terri lost her best friend and shopping buddy. Trina, who is a younger version of Bev, lost her mentor and mom.
- My son-in-law Steen Hudson, whose calls to check in with me were so encouraging and helpful.

- My grandson, Keaton Hudson, who mourned his grandmother and talked with me about the process - including a discussion regarding the possibility of remarriage.
- My son Todd, whose courage in facing his grief was - and is - an example to me. Through the pain of losing his mom, he has ministered to me while experiencing a journey of his own.

There is one more person in this journey. Caryl Taylor has been a friend for 30 years, to both Bev and I. She knew Bev and Bev knew her; we were in her home and she was in ours. Caryl was truly a friend in this journey and one day we discovered that something more than friendship had developed. She is now Caryl Goehner and has been my biggest fan in writing this book.

To all of you, thank you and God bless you. You will never know how greatly you have impacted my life. *To God be the glory!*

Don Goehner
San Jose, Calif.
October 2010

PART ONE
Ten Months and Ten Days

Celebrating Bev Goehner's final year

On November 10, 2006, Bev Goehner, my wife and childhood sweetheart, suddenly died. She was about to be released from Good Samaritan Hospital in San Jose, where she had been a patient for three days after suffering a seizure.

Looking back on the 10 months and 10 days Bev and I had together in 2006, I saw God's hand clearly and powerfully directing our path. We traveled a great deal and visited friends we had not seen in years. We attended our oldest grandson's junior high school graduation and our middle grandson's sixth-grade promotion.

There were wonderful times with business and ministry friends, as well as occasions when we simply relaxed in our love for one another. Our love was built on a shared love for God and nearly 50 years of marriage.

It was also a year in which Bev's memory issues continued to surface and we received a report from Stanford Hospital that was hard to accept. The diagnosis, mild cognitive impairment, meant they felt she was on the path to the dreaded disease that turns wonderful people into empty shells - Alzheimer's. The very same disease that victimized Bev's father for nearly a dozen years.

This is the chronicle of the journey Bev and I lived in 2006, a year that began without any hint that we were experiencing many things for the last time. Upon her death I entered a period of firsts which continues to this day. Journaling these events and feelings is one the hardest tasks I've ever undertaken. Often I need to stop and grieve. Now, even as I type, it is hard to believe she is not here with me in British Columbia at the lovely summer home on the Sunshine Coast where we spent many days in years past.

As you read, rejoice with me that Bev's pain is over. She is with her Heavenly Father, whom she loved and worshipped from childhood up to her last day on earth. Her godly reward is well deserved, having lived a life that echoed the words of her Savior, "Well done, good and faithful servant."

We loved being together and doing things together. Although my business and ministry commitments often had me on the road alone, when Bev was able to join me we visited colleagues, special friends, and beloved family members together. There were a few destinations and relationships that were very important to us as a couple, especially as Bev's health challenges increased.

Serving God and people as a couple

One of the biggest joys after Bev retired In 2000 from her 25-year ministry as a church-office administrator was that we could both attend Westmont College trustee functions in Santa Barbara. Prior to her retirement, she often could not go because of her church responsibilities.

She loved the Thursday-morning gatherings when the trustees and their spouses worshipped and prayed together. She told her friend, Vivian Nelson, on several occasions, "Bring your hankie. This is a special time."

She loved to hear about answered prayers, including those prayed for years by several Westmont trustees for our son, Todd, a 20-year prodigal.

The January 25-28, 2006, meetings gave her an additional opportunity to spend time with her grandsons and daughter, Trina, who live in Santa Barbara. Bev and Trina had always been close, but in recent months the phone calls had been less frequent. Bev looked forward to being in Santa Barbara in person.

The highlight of this trustees meeting was the special tribute given to Bruce Bare, former trustee; Roger Voskuyl, former president; and Roger Post, a former trustee and special friend. I was honored to present a tribute to Roger Post. "Bev remembered how brave Roger's wife, Sally, was after his death." We made arrangements to meet Sally for dinner in March. Little did any of us know that within a year I also would be attending those meetings as a widower.

Bev's final Westmont trustees meeting was May 3-7, a weekend which included commencement and the farewell dinner for outgoing president, Stan Gaede, and his wife, Judy. Judy and Bev were quite close; Bev so appreciated Judy's down-to-earth-style and love for people. Bev really treasured the official picture of the four of us, taken that evening.

On both of these occasions we drove home with great joy because the trustees and spouses were more than just a group of people supporting the same institution of higher learning. These were fellow Christians, authentic people and – something we came to increasingly value – our staunch prayer supporters.

One of the most difficult drives I have ever made was to the January 2007 trustees meeting. As I drove south, my emotions were raw. My eyes were filled with tears as I recalled the trips Bev and I made together, and some of the conversations and laughter we had enjoyed as we drove. It just didn't seem right that Bev was not accompanying me. I had gone alone to trustees meetings before, but I always could look forward to seeing my wife when I returned. Not this time.

I remember arriving at the home of my daughter and son-in-law in Santa Barbara, going into the guest room and realizing that I would never again share this special room with my sweetheart. Everything seemed wrong. It was awkward for the whole family as we begin to fully grasp that she was not coming back.

A loyal and supportive wife

When Bev and I married in 1958, we both felt called to ministry. I attended Westmont College with the express purpose of moving into some kind of ministry service. For the entire 48 years of our marriage, Bev was my partner and biggest supporter. I worked in a variety of ministry opportunities including Youth for Christ, Azusa Pacific College, Westmont College and, finally, The Goehner Group.

In 1990 I established The Goehner Group as a for-profit organization helping Christian ministries and churches.

Bev had her own ministry in church administration. We were both committed to reaching people, doing so in a spirit of compassion and service. In her retirement years, Bev traveled with me on many occasions, coming to love The Goehner Group's clients as I did.

The times we travelled and ministered together reminded me that Bev was more than a wife. She was my best friend and confidant. We shared everything – the good and the bad. Frankly, we raised each other and I still find myself thinking, "I need to call Bev and tell her…"

Simpson University

In 2004 I began consulting the leadership at Simpson. At the same time, Bev began connecting with the school her sister and brother-in-law attended, and where her father had served as a trustee.

Driving to Redding, Calif., together gave us time for conversation, as well as times when we just enjoyed each other silently. She loved being with me, and I with her - even if it was a work day. I loved having her along because, after all these years, our conversations were easy and very special. She also welcomed our drives to Simpson because she did not want me driving the four hours alone, especially at night.

While I worked with the university's staff and president, Bev shopped or just hung out in the president's office and talked with his assistants. One assistant, Carolyn, knew Bev's sister, Jene, quite well and was very welcoming to Bev. In fact, the entire Simpson community treated us with great kindness and accepted us as family. Bev loved being with these friends and kept insisting that her sister, and brother-in-law, Wes, meet us at Simpson to visit the new campus they'd never seen.

In 2006 we made five trips to Simpson during our 10 months together. The first, on January 12, had us going up and back the same day. We left early and Bev helped drive so we could be in Redding by 9 a.m. After she shopped in the morning, I picked her up for lunch and then she spent the afternoon visiting and reading in the president's office.

Our second visit was April 28-29, for commencement and the farewell dinner for outgoing president Dr. James Grant. Bev was especially drawn to Dr. Grant's wife, Hazel, remarking on how gracious Hazel had been.

Our third trip is probably the most meaningful to me at this point in my journey after Bev's death. We planned on visiting Weaverville, about 45 minutes west of Redding, to celebrate our anniversary, but my busy schedule required us to wait and drive up on June 28 (the actual date of our wedding anniversary) and return on the 30th. We ate our anniversary dinner at In-N-Out Burgers in Vacaville and Bev got a big kick out of that.

We decided during one of our planned summer trips we would set aside one of our special dinners to celebrate our anniversary.

It was during this trip that we discussed her upcoming test at Stanford University, conducted by a neurologist. We wanted to get a second opinion after a neurologist in San Jose indicated Bev was in the beginning stages of dementia.

Our fourth visit to Simpson came in late August, after Dr. Larry McKinney was chosen as the new president. We drove up on August 24 and enjoyed a special dinner with the president's staff. I worked on Friday with the president and the advancement staff, then Bev and I headed home in the late afternoon.

This trip followed our visit to Washington state for our 50-year high-school reunions, and was prior to our upcoming ocean cruise with friends from Mount Hermon Christian Conference Center. Our conversation centered on those events.

My final visit to Simpson with my wife was October 12-14, just four weeks before her death. During the weekend, Larry McKinney was inaugurated as Simpson's new president, and I worked with the trustees and the foundation board on the upcoming capital campaign. Bev was disappointed her sister and brother-in-law could not attend, but her time with the new president's wife, Debbie, was a highlight.

Because of Bev's love for Simpson, we (I, along with her sister and brother-in-law) established a scholarship in her honor.

Our family

God blessed us with three children – Terri, Todd and Trina. We not only chose all "Ts," but their middle names all begin with an

"L". Like many parents who are thrilled with the names they chose for their kids, we heard quite a bit about those two letters of the alphabet from the children as they got older!

Bev and I came from quite different family backgrounds. I was one of 32 grandchildren, all of whom lived in two small adjacent communities in Central Washington. We were very close and every Christmas Eve was spent at my paternal grandfather's home (because it was his birthday). Bev's family was not close - she did not even know some of her cousins. After we married she quickly adopted the Goehner family as her own.

Our goal was to have a family that loved being together and, for the most part, we succeeded. Bev made certain we celebrated every birthday and the holidays with one another; Thanksgiving and Christmas were always extra special.

At present, Trina is the only one who has married. She and Steen, my son-in-law, blessed us with three grandsons: Keaton, Taylor and Carter. Early on, Bev and I were determined to be active grandparents. Bev was born to be a mom and especially a grandmother; she succeeded admirably at both.

Family milestones

For two consecutive Thursdays, Bev and I traveled to Santa Barbara to watch our two oldest grandsons achieve milestones. On June 15, in 90-degree heat, we watched Keaton Hudson's graduation ceremony at La Colina Junior High. Keaton was one of the valedictorians and Bev was very proud of her first-born grandson. Later, we went to lunch at the Enterprise Fish Company and she thoroughly enjoyed the special occasion.

One week later we were at Hope Elementary School to witness the promotion of sixth graders, including Keaton's brother, Taylor. In his typical style, Taylor did not tell anyone he was going to lead the Pledge of Allegiance. As he quietly approached the microphone and began the pledge, Bev beamed! Taylor's achievements always thrilled his "Nama" because he was often in the shadow of his older brother, Keaton.

Bev left Santa Barbara with mixed emotions. She thoroughly enjoyed both events but she did not feel she was connecting with our daughter, Trina as she had in the past. On this second trip she even shed some tears. Although it was very unusual for Bev to cry, I began to see this behavior more and more during her final months as her confusion increased.

Connecting with friends and family

The Florida connection

Bev and I made two trips to Florida in 2006, one in February for my work and visits with friends, and one in April that combined a Young Life national meeting, time with friends, and business endeavors.

During the February trip we had dinner with Keith and Karen Wright in Orlando. Keith was at that time executive pastor of First Presbyterian Church in Orlando and Karen is a vice president of Compassion International. Several years ago, during the time our son-in-law, Steen Hudson, was a resident director in one of the Westmont dormitories, Karen served as a resident assistant. The Wrights are a wonderful young couple and the four of us had a great evening together.

I worked on First Presbyterian's capital campaign before we departed for Sanibel Island and a visit with Keith and Nini Sieck. Bev had never been to the western side of Florida and she enjoyed our drive to the Sieck's beautiful home on the golf course.

We had a marvelous weekend and it is a fond memory of 2006. We talked, laughed, ate, drove around the island and worshipped together during our three-day visit. Although it was our first time together as couples, we felt completely at ease. Little did we know this would our one and only visit.

The Carolinas and Florida

We arrived in Greenville, S.C. (the site of our Young Life Capernaum Committee national meetings), on Thursday evening, April 20, and stayed at a nice hotel downtown. It was Bev's first visit to the deep South and she loved the Young Life staff and committee.

We had a great weekend, with the Friday meetings culminating in an evening at a Capernaum Club. Bev had always been a bit uncomfortable around disabled youth, but she loved this experience and really saw how God was working in these kids' hearts.

Following the Saturday-morning meeting, we spent the afternoon exploring the city, including Bob Jones University. Both of us had heard about BJU for years, but it was fun to actually be on campus. We laughed about our visit to a campus where all the girls were in skirts and the men wore long pants. Most visitors, however, were in shorts and cut-offs! It was an interesting contrast.

Later that afternoon we walked around downtown and discovered a street fair. When it began to rain, we ducked into an ice-cream shop and enjoyed our large cones while watching the rain.

It was so much fun watching Bev in these kinds of settings. She came alive, particularly because she had me to herself. Bev made a huge sacrifice throughout our marriage, sharing me with the people

I encountered in my ministry leadership roles and business contacts. So, for that reason and dozens of others, our Saturday afternoon in the rain was special, one of my most-prized memories from 2006.

Early that evening we met Bobby and Marian Austell for dinner. This was a delightful evening and one Bev enjoyed and talked about often. It was great to get to know this couple better as we experienced the wonders of southern hospitality. Although the four of us agreed to reunite at the fall meeting of Young Life Capernaum in November, we didn't have that opportunity; Bev died on the Friday afternoon those Dallas meetings began.

Leaving Greenville for Asheville, N. C., we embarked on a beautiful drive, stopping at the N.C. border to get help to find and book a room for the night. I was able to make a reservation at the Inn at the Biltmore, part of the Vanderbilt family complex.

It was a night to remember! Our room was bigger than our townhouse at home and we were waited on from start to finish. Visiting the Biltmore was a wonderful experience, but Bev got tired quickly and I had to explore some of the rooms by myself. Her fatigue was another result of her increasing pain and inability to do things – things that had been very natural and easy for her in the past.

After enjoying a delicious ice cream cone, we visited and marveled at the Biltmore's beautiful gardens. Our restaurant that evening, the Steak House, was a special treat because we rarely ate red meat. Our lodging package included the Inn's Southern Buffet Breakfast. Not only was there an incredible abundance of wonderful food, we were almost embarrassed by the amount we consumed! Throughout our time in Asheville we heard lots of laughs and comments about how our West-Coast speech lacked the correct accent for the South!

While still in the Asheville area, we visited several spots of interest. The first was Montreat College, connected to Montreat Conference Center and part of the Presbyterian Church U.S.A. The visit had additional importance because I was following up with the president of Montreat, who was one of Westmont's potential presidential candidates.

Our next stop was at Windy Gap, the Young Life camp that has had a tremendous impact in the southeastern United States.

Our third visit was to the Billy Graham Conference Center at The Cove. This was an awesome experience and one I will never forget. Bev and I had a wonderful guided tour, ending in the Prayer Room where our host knelt with us and prayed. Finally, we stopped by The Southern Baptist conference center, LifeWay Ridgecrest, (and a client of The Goehner Group at the time).

Arriving in Raleigh, N. C., that evening, we visited our longtime friends Dwight and Marilyn Jordan. Dwight was our family's doctor when we lived in Southern Calif. and he served on the Youth for Christ board of directors. Marilyn and Bev were Pioneer Girls leaders at our church during that time. We had not seen them since their daughter, Valerie, was married in 1976.

What a marvelous evening we experienced with these dear folks. We went to dinner together and then had dessert back at their home, laughing and chatting the evening away. This encounter was one of the many divine appointments we experienced and were grateful for in 2006. Bev was so energized by this visit and talked about it the remainder of her time on earth.

We weren't finished quite yet. On Tuesday morning, we flew to Orlando and spent the afternoon at Sea World. We remembered taking our children to Sea World in San Diego years before, but this time we were the ones having a fun day acting like little kids – kids who were in love and loved being with one another. The Bev I knew best – laughing, talking and enjoying her "Donnie" – was with me again.

On Wednesday I spent the morning working with leaders from First Presbyterian of Orlando, following up on their capital-campaign project before we flew home that afternoon.

Bev's request

On Sunday afternoon, March 12, we drove to Monterey to meet Sally Post. Her husband, Roger was probably one of my two best friends and colleagues on the Westmont College board of trustees. During board meetings our mission often seemed to be to keep things light, even during intense discussion and decision-making sessions. We would work at making the other person laugh during meetings. One of the notes I passed to Roger caused him to laugh out loud at an inappropriate moment. He received weird looks from the other trustees, ensuring that he would never completely forgive me.

His death, on November 9, 2005, was a huge blow to me. Despite being a non-smoker, he had been diagnosed with lung cancer and three weeks later was dead. I was very disappointed I could not attend his memorial service because I was in Nepal on a mission trip with our church.

Following Roger's death, Sally told us she wanted to stay in touch, so we made the trip to Monterey and met her. At the columbarium where Roger's ashes were placed, we remembered the great things about him, the relationship between Roger and me, and the friendship between the two couples.

As we drove to dinner, Bev was very quiet and then said, "I think this would be a good place for our ashes someday." In just nine months, "someday" became a reality.

I knew exactly what I needed to do after her death. Prior to Bev's memorial service on November 18, I drove to Monterey and bought a double niche, next to Roger and Sally's. There was a single niche in between those of the two families, which I purchased for my single daughter, Terri.

Sally and I have often joked since then that her husband is pleading with God to send Jesus back before I die. He is willing to spend eternity in heaven with me but having our ashes side by side is a little much for Roger. He can relax, though, because Bev's ashes are closer to Roger's than mine will be!

At the time, Bev's request seemed innocuous, but it became very significant because it made my task of choosing a site so much easier. The Monterey City Cemetery has since become a place of comfort and refuge to our family – especially for our son, Todd. Those visits were a major part of his grief journey. Once again, God knew what was best and went before us.

Our favorite getaway and time with special friends

In 1984, Bev and I discovered Cambria (or Cambria Pines by the Sea, its name from an earlier time), a small community on the central Calif. coast that quickly became our favorite getaway during our years in Southern Calif. and after our move to the Bay Area.

Cambria is just a three-hour drive from San Jose and we have visited almost yearly. This quiet community is a haven for artists, with many locally owned shops that are fun to visit, great restaurants (no fast-food places) and wonderful Moonstone Beach, facing the Pacific Ocean. It's a quick walk across the road and down to the beach to watch the tide change and the sea otters as they play and rest in the sun on the rocky beach.

On May 19 we drove south to Cambria where we met our travel companions and friends, Tom and Viv Nelson. We had been extremely compatible, travelling together throughout Calif., the western states, and Canada. Bev and Viv were great friends and loved to talk, especially about their grandchildren. Our adventures included Bev nearly being arrested at the Canadian border when she got out of the car and used her body language to complain about the long wait! When I got involved, things became even more complicated. Tom and Viv have never forgotten…or stopped laughing.

During the weekend I was aware that Bev was having trouble with her memory, but I don't think Tom and Viv knew. My wife had gotten very adept at asking me the kinds of questions that gave her answers to things she had forgotten. To this day, I am convinced that she was aware of her memory issues long before they became apparent to me.

A major part of my grief journey was learning not to dwell on the what-ifs, such as why we didn't seek medical help earlier. I realize, of course, there is nothing I can do to change the circumstances. The pain of coming to grips with no longer sharing vacations with friends and just enjoying life as a couple was, at times, very difficult. I have missed her terribly and yet life was going on around me. .

The four of us concluded our weekend, agreeing to plan a 2007 vacation together. As it turned out, I did have a long weekend with Tom and Viv in December 2007, the same vacation weekend Bev and I discussed having with the Nelsons as we drove home that Monday. By that December, more than a year after becoming a widower, I had become accustomed to be a single man with couples, and concentrated on the positive, rather than having a pity party.

Orange County visits and reunions

Bev and I lived in Southern Calif. for nearly 30 years and spent approximately one third of that time in the Long Beach/Orange County area. We made many friends and have great memories of the area in which our children grew into their teenage years. It was also a time of shifting from a parachurch youth ministry to college administration and fundraising.

The first weekend of June we flew to Orange County to investigate the potential purchase of a time-share at a Marriott Resort in Newport Beach. At the resort we listened to the sales presentation and although the offer was appealing, I explained that we were facing some family health problems and needed to clarify those before we could make any type of financial commitment. Bev was a little upset with me because she didn't understand that the "health problems" were her memory issues.

We walked through Newport Fashion Plaza, drove down the coast to Dana Point and enjoyed our spacious room. The entire weekend was a totally relaxing break from my hectic schedule.

On Saturday evening we drove to Laguna Beach and had dinner with Gary and Peg Low, longtime friends. Gary was my business mentor and boss when I worked at Azusa Pacific University in the mid-1970s. I did additional work with him after I became an independent contractor and I am very grateful for his contribution to my life. I've had several mentors in my professional life, but Gary was by far the most influential.

During dinner, we shared the medical journey on which we had embarked after receiving the initial diagnosis of Bev's dementia. The doctor had recommended we get a second opinion from specialists at Stanford Hospital. After asking Gary and Peg to join with our prayer team of close friends, they readily agreed to pray and uphold us on this journey. It was hard for Bev to hear me reveal the information about her condition – as well as share deeply about our fears – with others, but she agreed that we needed as many people praying as possible.

The next day we had lunch with my sister, Eldora, and shared a similar message and request. Later that afternoon we stopped to visit Nancy Jensen, a classmate of ours at Westmont. She and her husband, Jim (also a Westmont alum) were part of a small-group Bible study in which we participated for several years. At one point the Goehners and Jensens had season tickets to Long Beach State basketball games.

This was a special visit because we had lost contact with Nancy after Jim died in 1995. The conversation on this beautiful spring day was uplifting as we felt like we had picked up where we had left off years before.

Nancy and Jim had a great influence on my professional life in 1979, when I told them I was going to seek a position as a college president. These two close friends told me gently but firmly, "Don, you don't have the personality makeup or patience for that job!" It was wonderful (as well as accurate and wise) advice and saved me years of fruitless searching.

That evening we met our son, Todd, and his fiancée at the time, Charlene, for dinner near the Los Angeles airport. Todd had been our prodigal, but his life had turned around and our relationship with him seemed brand-new. We had a wonderful evening of food and conversation. Bev always called Todd "my favorite son" (he was her only son!) and was animated in talking about Todd as we drove back to our hotel.

Just a month later, we returned to Orange County and attended the 50th wedding anniversary celebration of Gary and Peg Low. On the evening of July 3 we saw friends we had not seen for a long time, some for as long as 20 years. It was a fun evening and Bev seemed to really enjoy herself during the cruise, dinner, and interactions with people. After Bev's death, some friends shared they noticed some differences in her behavior that night. But like most people, they did not comment to me because they felt it might be a one-time occurrence.

That same evening, Bev told Gary she was concerned about her relationship with Trina, our youngest daughter. Bev thought they had grown somewhat apart. In hindsight, I think Trina and Bev had indeed grown a little apart (over no particular incident), but Bev's memory issues caused her to be anxious in ways I had not experienced with her before.

Looking back on these two Southern Calif. trips, I realized these were the last times several people close to us, including my sister, saw Bev alive. It was a special blessing to see Gary and Peg twice in such a short time, and we were so pleased to be back in contact with Nancy. God used several of those people, especially Nancy, to minister to me after Bev's death. Once again, God went before us and prepared the way!

Client trips as a couple

As I stated earlier, a benefit of Bev's retirement was her ability to travel with me to client locations throughout the United States.

On January 3, 2006, we traveled to Bakersfield where I conducted training sessions for Laurelglen Bible Church's capital campaign. Bev sat in on the training and met the pastors' wives. On our drive home we talked for almost four hours solid. She remarked about how special this time was – having me to herself, with no people around and no phone calls.

Bev made it clear to me then – and throughout that year - my business travel routine was wearing thin. She needed more of me. When asked about my regrets following her death, this conversation comes instantly to mind. Bev shared her husband with the world of Christian ministry and paid a price for it. But I paid a price as well. Nevertheless, I believe one of her heavenly rewards is this gift of hers to the body of Christ.

In addition to attending Mount Hermon Conference Center's Capital Campaign Gala in Sacramento in early 2006, we spent most of the weekend together alone. Mount Hermon was one of those rare clients, a group of people with whom we had both a thoroughly professional and deeply personal relationship.

Bev enjoyed the events and helped in any way she could, but by this last Gala she was tired, and simply sat and watched. Her back was in constant pain, even though she was an amazingly brave woman with a high tolerance for pain. Our doctor pointed out later, "Her body fell apart in 2006." But I'm afraid I missed some signs of deterioration early that year.

One of my greatest losses, beginning in late 2006, has been travelling to work with clients and attending all kinds of events without Bev. My widower status was more pronounced – and painful – at these times, than at any other.

Entering a room, sitting down with clients or joining an activity with others, I always felt I was escorting the most beautiful woman. Plus, I knew she saw me as her hero and was always my biggest booster. I miss those times and particularly her prayers for me, the clients, and the events.

Final visits, vacations and reunions

Bev's boys

In mid-July we drove to Southern Calif. to spend a weekend with our family. Bev was very anxious to see our grandsons. Prior to her retirement she would often leave work on Friday evening when I was on the road for business and drive the five hours to Santa Barbara to see the three grandsons. Little did we know this mid-summer visit would be the last time she would see Keaton, our oldest grandson.

In late October, three weeks before Bev died, we made a quick trip to Santa Barbara to watch Taylor and Carter play soccer. Keaton was away and at the time his absence did not seem significant. Later, though, I realized that she did not see him once during the last four months of her life. Keaton was special because he was her first. He was bald for the first year of his life, which endeared him to her. I can't count the number of trips she made to Santa Barbara during that first year!

During that weekend, we had breakfast with our son, Todd. Driving home, Bev remarked on the progress Todd was making and how much she missed spending more time with him. Because of his responsibilities during 2006, Bev only saw him on two or three occasions – something Todd has regretted ever since. But on this October morning we enjoyed great conversation, laughter and discussion about his upcoming visit with us on Thanksgiving.

Our time with Todd was yet another reminder that God is in the "small stuff" (as my friend, Bruce Bickel and his co-author, Stan Janz, said in one their books).

The highlight of Bev's last year

For more than a year we had anticipated a 10-day period in late July and early August when our high school would celebrate their 50-year reunions.

Bev and I met in January 1956, shortly after I came to Christ. The person who was discipling me at the time invited me to share my testimony at the Wenatchee (Wash.) Christian and Missionary Alliance Church. I met Bev after the service, and she always said that I didn't let go when we shook hands! My first vivid remembrance is one month after meeting each other, this attractive brunette with lots of energy was in charge. She got my attention and our first date was a few weeks later.

We flew out of San Jose on Thursday evening, August 27, for Dryden, Wash., a village of 150 (and my hometown). As always, we stayed with my uncle and aunt, Walt and Alvina Goehner. To this day, they call their guest room "Don and Bev's room."

Because the school districts in Dryden and Peshastin (a nearby town) had eventually consolidated into one, the two schools held a combined 50th graduation reunion for the last class in each high school. In 1957, Peshastin-Dryden, or PD, High School was born. That meant that Wes and Jene Jeske, Bev's sister and brother-in-law would be at the same reunion. We had a great weekend and Bev enjoyed my reunion immensely because she knew so many of the people. None of us knew at the time that this would be the next-to-last time Bev and her sister would be together.

After Bev's death, Jene told me during that reunion, for the first time, she noticed Bev's memory issues. Bev told Jene on three occasions she was going to get a piece of pie for her but never came back with it. Jene, like others, wasn't sure if she should say anything.

We laughed and talked about our dating days, as well as interacting with people we had not seen in as many as 30 years. It was hard to say goodbye on Sunday, but we were now looking forward to Bev's reunion the following weekend in Wenatchee, 15 miles east and the commercial hub of Central Washington. Bev called it the "big city" (its population is still less than 30,000).

Between the two reunions we drove to Whidbey Island in Puget Sound, where we had spent many happy days of vacationing, particularly in the last few years. Our favorite place was the Saratoga Inn, one of several bed-and-breakfast Inns managed by our friends, Roger and Sally Post. (Whenever Roger found out I was staying at one of his inns, he would call and admonish me, "Don't steal the towels.") Bev and I ate at our favorite restaurant and shopped at an often-visited jewelry store, where we bought her a bracelet.

On Thursday, August 3, we drove over the Cascade Mountains to Wenatchee. After checking into our hotel, we met Ardelle and Lee Temanson (from Minneapolis). Bev and Ardelle had been best friends in high school, and this friendship had continued for 50 years. The ladies spoke regularly by phone and e-mailed one another occasionally. With Bev's permission, I quietly shared with Ardelle my concerns about my wife's memory.

The next few days were marvelous as these two ladies relished their time together and with classmates whom they had not seen in quite some time. I was thrilled because this reunion was the highlight of her year. She had been to two previous events and had come away somewhat disappointed. But not this time.

She was as animated as I had seen her in months. She talked with lots of classmates as they shared stories of their lives, families and, in particular, their grandchildren. Bev's entire countenance changed when the topic focused on her boys – Carter, Keaton, and Taylor. Out came the pictures, the stories and the priceless anecdotes.

A highlight that weekend happened when Bev shared with her classmate, Trina Hansen Adams, that she had named her second daughter after her. Trina Adams shared with me at the Wenatchee memorial for Bev, in January 2007, how meaningful that conversation was to her and how honored she was to have our daughter named after her.

Bev was thrilled by the number of classmates who had become Christians in recent years, and I was delighted my dear wife was blessed by people who expressed their deep respect for her. Trina Adams said to me at the memorial service, "Bev became the woman we all wanted to be."

As I said goodbye to Ardelle, she whispered in my ear, "Take care of my friend. She is approaching a dark time." How prophetic these words were.

A last visit with her sister

In the early fall of 2006, I had to make a quick one-day (up-and-back) trip to the Seattle area. I invited Bev to go along and visit with her sister while I visited with my client. As I dropped Bev off, we agreed to meet that afternoon at a restaurant just off I-5 in Everett, before for our trip back to the airport and our flight home.

When I arrived at the restaurant, Wes, Jene, and Bev began to walk into the restaurant. Wes asked what time our flight was scheduled to depart and when I replied 7:30, he said," We don't have time for dinner." I said, "Who said we were having dinner? I just wanted us to meet so we could get to the airport." Bev got a sheepish look and said she misunderstood. We all laughed and got in separate cars. Jene's final comment was, "That would be something Bev would do."

My sweetie had a history of misunderstanding things. However, as we drove away, I was crying inwardly because I knew this was different. Bev had forgotten and looked completely confused when I reminded her that we had discussed the meeting time, place and purpose in detail. As we drove south toward the airport, I was again reminded of the issues we faced and asked God for courage and grace. Despite the confusion, I am grateful the sisters had a last day together.

Our final vacation

On Friday, September 22, Bev and I flew to Montreal to embark on a Fall Colors Cruise sponsored by Mount Hermon Christian Conference Center. This was a first for us. We had never been on a cruise and weren't certain how we would react. I had always felt cruises were for the rich and retired, and we almost backed out in the last two weeks because of the pressures of my work. After concluding we would not get any money back if we cancelled, we went.

The flight was a travel nightmare. We were delayed out of San Jose and it was apparent we would miss our connection in Chicago. O'Hare is not my favorite airport and I was grumbling about our situation. When we arrived in Chicago we discovered we would not miss our connection because all flights were delayed and we would be waiting for some time. We finally boarded the flight and almost immediately an electrical storm hit with a fury I have rarely seen.

Because of the danger to workers, the tarmac was evacuated and the 50 passengers on our plane were isolated on board during the storm. The rain came at us sideways and the entire plane shook. People around us began to pray and I was not certain that small regional jetliner could withstand the buffeting of the wind and precipitation.

Bev, who was a nervous flyer to begin with, was quite frightened - and we hadn't even departed!

It was an hour before the storm subsided and the crew got back on the plane. The storm caused further delays and we finally arrived in Montreal at 11 p.m., five hours late. After a short night of sleep, we took a taxi to the ship, The Rotterdam, and began an adventure I will always treasure.

We had a great time as the ship made its way up the St. Lawrence Seaway to Quebec City, and eventually to the open sea. For seven days we enjoyed visits to shore in Quebec City, the Maritime Provinces and Bar Harbor, Maine. We feasted on great food; listened to longtime-friend Bob Kraning share the Word of God; enjoyed Buddy Greene's music and worship leadership; and spent time with friends.

I have always been a practical joker and so on the first night, I asked our waiters to sing "Happy Birthday" to Bev. (It was not really her birthday, but the waiters didn't know). Bev was a good sport and went along with the gag and enjoyed her special dessert. What I did not know was that this would be the last time we would sing that song to my sweetheart. On December 22, when I observed the birth date that we shared – and just three months after her shipboard "birthday" – I realized she had indeed celebrated her 68th. Just a little prematurely.

There were highs and lows during our time on the cruise. The highs were the time we could spend together as a couple and the joy of a vacation without a phone. We loved Nova Scotia and relished our visit to an art and craft show at an Anglican church where we were served tea and crumpets. Bev was delighted with the gentlemen who played the bagpipes on the dock in Sydney upon our arrival; I have a picture of him and Bev. Shortly after the picture was taken, she called her sister, Jene, and they spoke fondly of their mother's love of this style of music.

During the cruise, we got to spend an entire morning with Bob and Carol Kraning. Bob and I were contemporaries in the ministry of Youth for Christ in the 1960s and we had not been together as couples for more than 30 years. The conversation was stimulating and we had the opportunity to be brought up to date on our children, grandchildren, and our health.

Bev, in her typical humble fashion, said she was surprised Carol remembered her. She'd forgot we'd been together at many YFC staff conferences and that Bev had spoken at one such conference about the role of a YFC staff wife. (By the way, she was funny, witty and good, and received a big ovation.)

Another long conversation took place with a couple who were recently married. Ben had been married for many years to a lady who was involved in ministry with Bev when we lived in Ventura in the 1960s. Carol had never been married but was someone I knew through my Westmont connections. We enjoyed our time and Bev was delighted that Ben had found a woman who loved him so and was taking care of him due to his health issues.

The best parts of the trip were the conversations we had lying in bed, walking on the ship's deck and visiting ashore. It was one of our best vacations and we agreed to take another cruise in the near future.

But there were storm clouds on the horizon. I became aware she did not want me out of her sight. Twice, when I had to run errands, she wanted to remain in the cabin because I would know where to find her. Each time, I assured her I would return promptly and did. Each time, she had tears in her eyes.

When we arrived in Boston, we had to wait on the dock for some friends to pick us up. There was no bench on which to sit near where we had to wait. Bev's back was in constant pain and I found a bench across the parking lot from where I was standing for her to rest until our hosts arrived. I walked back to my original site and in less than five minutes, a fearful Bev suddenly appeared at my side. I became keenly aware that this experience had been frightening and I could not do that again. My thought was, Lord help me to be more sensitive to her needs in these kinds of situations.

Our hosts, Stan and Judy Gaede, arrived and we headed off to their home in Wenham, Mass., for an afternoon of sightseeing, a leisurely dinner, and a great evening of conversation. Stan had recently rejoined the administration and leadership team of Gordon College, after serving at Westmont for 10 years (five as provost and five as president). Judy had always been a gracious friend to Bev and we thoroughly enjoyed our time. On Sunday, we attended Park Street Church together and enjoyed brunch prior to going to our hotel on the waterfront.

It turned out to be our last special dinner together. We all went to a wonderful restaurant next to the hotel, a spot where we had eaten several years before.

On Monday, we had planned on sightseeing in Boston with folks we met on the cruise, but Bev begged off; she told me later she just wanted to be with me. As Bev's memory failed and her physical pain increased, she became quieter and more reflective, wanting to be with only me more and more. I confess I was dense and did not always get it. In fact, some of this I did not totally comprehend until she was gone.

We did wander across the street to Quincy Market and I helped her buy a cute pair of shoes. Bev loved shoes. Our kids nicknamed her

"Imelda" after a certain Filipino first lady. It is a pair she never wore because her feet swelled in the final weeks of her life. They are the one pair I have saved, giving the rest to an agency that assists women who want to get back in to the workforce.

Darkening days

Testing and a disturbing diagnosis

It is hard to remember when I first began to see changes in Bev; perhaps in late 2003 or early 2004. It was little things at first: forgetting what she had just said or forgetting she had previously told me something.

At first I felt I was imagining things and dismissed it. But as her struggles became more common, I talked with my pastor who suggested I talk to my doctor about it.

I probably waited almost a year before I shared my concerns with Dr. Ed DeWees. He asked me to describe the symptoms I was observing. When I finished, he looked at me seriously and said, "She has all the indications of Alzheimer's. We need to get her tested. Please call her doctor (his partner) and make an appointment."

I went back to my office in a daze. What did this mean? I didn't believe Bev would agree to the test because her dad had had the disease, and she knew the downsides.

I called Linda, my assistant, into my office and explained what I had just heard and asked if she had observed anything unusual. She replied that generally, she hadn't, but there were one or two times when Bev's statements surprised her.

Linda encouraged me to make an appointment, which I did. However, I called back and cancelled the appointment because I felt Bev needed to be part of our planning. It took several weeks before

I could broach the subject with her. Not surprisingly, Bev didn't see the need. In looking back on that conversation, I realized that her dementia was far enough advanced at this point that normal cognitive decisions were becoming very difficult. It was in early 2006 – several months after my appointment – that Bev met with her doctor and agreed to be tested.

I will never know what happened during that appointment, but Bev was not tested and seemed confused by what the doctor had told her. By this time I was getting frustrated because I saw her decreased capacity to reason and increased confusion. One of the complicating factors was that Bev firmly believed she had always had a learning disability and, had she been born two generations later, would have received special attention, including tutoring. This also caused me to downplay the seriousness of my concerns.

Exasperated, I visited my doctor in May and explained what was happening. Or, more accurately, what was not happening. He immediately swung into action, requesting that Bev be transferred to his care and setting up an appointment with a neurologist.

In early June, the neurologist put Bev through a series of tests. It was difficult for me to be there because she was answering his questions incorrectly. After an hour, he told us his initial diagnosis: Bev was experiencing the early stages of dementia. He would not call it Alzheimer's because more testing was needed. Bev did not say anything, but her body shook next to mine as she heard the diagnosis. And, this was only the first of several such appointments, with bad news coming out of each one. He ordered an MRI and gave us the option of receiving a second opinion from Stanford Hospital's neurology department.

Soon after that I had a conversation with each of my three

children and asked if they had noticed any changes in their mom's actions. Each one said yes, they had, particularly during Christmas 2005. Like others who had observed Bev's changed behavior, they were reluctant to discuss it with me or anyone else. Those witnessing changes didn't want to say anything, in case it was just a one-time occurrence and not something more serious.

We went back to our doctor and arranged for a second-opinion appointment with Dr. Greicius, the head of neurology at Stanford. In the meantime, the MRI showed no signs of Alzheimer's. We were ecstatic! I immediately e-mailed the news to a small circle of friends we had asked to pray, and talked about the answers we hoped to receive at the upcoming appointment at Stanford Hospital.

On July 21, we met with a neurologist who talked with us and tested Bev. After approximately 30 minutes, Dr. Greicius joined us. Again, it was so hard to watch Bev give the wrong answers to fairly simple questions, like, "What day of the week is it today?" She answered, "Thursday" and my heart sank. It was Friday.

My eyes were moist as the doctor began talking to her, indicating she had all the symptoms of moderate cognitive impairment. When questioned, Dr. Greicius conveyed it might be the beginning of Alzheimer's or that her condition might remain as it was for the rest of her life. He was clear, however, that things would not improve.

I asked how they would know if it was moving toward Alzheimer's and he replied that time was the key factor. We just had to wait and see. He concluded by saying they would like to conduct neuropsychological tests to further assess her situation. The first appointment was October 10, after we returned from our cruise.

I was grateful that the size of our prayer team had increased, because the e-mail I sent that Friday evening was filled with the discouragement Bev and I both felt. During the 10 weeks between appointments, we rarely discussed the subject. I think we were both in some form of denial. Bev was certain the diagnosis would change; I wanted to be as positive as possible.

On October 10 we spent most of the day at Stanford. I was not allowed in the room where Bev was tested, but was questioned at length by the neuropsychologist. At the end of the day, Bev was exhausted. When I asked her how she did, she replied, "I think I did well but it was very hard." We were told to return October 20 to receive the results.

Fortunately, we had two busy weeks and didn't have time to dwell on the potential results. On Friday, October 20, we drove to Stanford Hospital. As we sat and waited for the doctor, we held hands and I sensed that Bev was perspiring. I could not imagine what my beautiful, high-school sweetheart was thinking and feeling.

Dr. Chin gave us a fairly thorough report, telling us Bev had done well on two sections of the test and there was no reason she couldn't drive. I felt her body exhale. On the three sections of the test that measured cognitive responses, however, she had done poorly.

The diagnosis echoed what Dr. Greicius had said in July. Mild cognitive impairment, with one significant difference: he was quite certain Bev's condition was headed towards Alzheimer's. Bev began to cry quietly and my eyes filled with tears. There it was, that dreaded word, Alzheimer's. And Bev was moving ever closer toward it.

We walked out of the office in shock, under a cloud of sadness. I held Bev as she cried quietly and we walked to our car. I must add, even then, God went before us and walked behind us; we were scheduled to drive to Santa Barbara in the early evening to watch our two youngest grandsons play soccer the next morning. After stopping for ice cream, we drove home and quickly packed to leave for Santa Barbara. Although we visited several times a year, it was probably the toughest drive to this city we had ever experienced. We stopped in Santa Maria, 65 miles north of Santa Barbara, and stayed overnight. I don't know if either of us slept.

On the way to Santa Maria, I spoke with each of our three children to explain the doctor's report. It was sobering news and they all received it differently, with responses ranging from near silence to, "Are you sure?'

Making the most of the time

One last visit to Santa Barbara

On Saturday, October 21, we arrived in time for an 8 a.m. soccer game. I will never forget how Bev's countenance changed. As soon as she saw Carter, our youngest grandson, she broke into a big grin. All at once, Carter began their long-established routine by asking, "Nama, rub my back." She happily complied and the two of them spent a wonderful hour together.

One of my weaknesses, I have to admit, is that I am a sports nut. More than that, watching my grandsons play is a special, almost spiritual, moment. On this morning, Bev was paying no attention to Taylor's game and I scolded her for not watching.

I wish I could take those words back, because she *was* paying attention to the most important activity: spending time with her youngest grandson. Incidentally, Carter looks and acts just like Bev. When we look at him, we see Bev in a male body. What a gift!

In the few hours between games, the family went to lunch and then gathered at the home of Carter's parents, Steen and Trina. I grabbed a nap (I knew I had to drive back that night) while Trina and Bev sat in lawn chairs and talked in the front yard.

Bev told me on the way home it was best conversation they had had that year. Yet another example of God going before us and allowing Bev one last opportunity to interact with her youngest daughter, the one who in appearance and temperament is so much like her mom.

The ride home was very hard because I was tired and became very sleepy. I could not let Bev take the wheel because she was having trouble driving. The previous night she pulled off the freeway when I was asleep and was about to enter a military base, thinking we had arrived in Santa Barbara.

Going public

On Sunday, I broached a very sensitive subject with Bev. I asked permission to share the diagnosis with the entire Westmont board of trustees. Some members were already part of our prayer team, but were unaware of our situation.

The Westmont board is unique, very much like a part of our extended family. We worship together before every trustees meeting and we have prayed for each other for years. I am absolutely convinced my son, Todd, is in the Kingdom and serving Christ because of the prayers of Westmont's trustees and their spouses.

My reason for wanting to share the news of Bev's condition and our needs was straightforward: we needed all the prayer we could get. And, if Bev's condition worsened, as the doctor indicated it likely would, I wanted people to know why her behavior was changing. My dear wife, in a moment of great courage, agreed to let me send an e-mail to the board.

The response was overwhelmingly positive. When I arrived for the trustees meeting, on Wednesday evening of that week, I was immediately surrounded by people who cared and were praying for us.

I went alone because Bev attended our church's women's retreat, which was coordinated by our daughter, Terri. Even though Bev did not especially enjoy retreats, she wanted to support her daughter, who was attempting to change the emphasis and quality of these retreats.

When Bev and I reunited on Sunday, October 29, she was very positive about Terri's leadership and the retreat, but confided she would never attend another one because she had sometimes become lost. (Looking at the picture of the women at the retreat, I almost didn't recognize Bev, with her vacant stare and confused look. She had no smile and there was no sparkle in her eyes.)

I told her about all the prayers and best wishes from the trustees and their spouses. "I got lots of hugs," I said, "that were meant for you." I even brought back some lovely gifts, including a beautiful scarf which she never had the opportunity to wear.

Our last road trip together and the beginning of the end

On Monday afternoon, October 30, we drove to Lake Tahoe to visit a Presbyterian conference center for which I had consulted on a capital campaign, and where I was to speak at a national leadership conference. On the drive, Bev was quite confused and asked several times where we were going.

In bed that night, she turned to me and said, "Why are you so worried about me?"

"Because, Honey, you asked me five times on the way here where we were going."

She was quiet and then said, "I did?"

"Yes, honey, you did."

She got very quiet and I sensed she was crying; I know I was.

As I lay in bed in the darkness that night, I remembered what had happened just a week earlier. I returned home from the office and could not find Bev. I panicked because one of our previous neighbors, an Alzheimer's patient, had wandered away and it was several hours before the police found her.

I walked to Terri's condo across the way, but Bev was not there and the door was locked. While returning to our home, I found her wandering down the walkway in tears. I hugged her and asked what was wrong.

"I have lost my key."

"What key?"

"The key to the mailbox."

We retraced her steps to the mailbox but couldn't find the key. Thinking she might have left the key at Terri's condo when she visited there earlier that afternoon, we walked back to our house to get the key to Terri's place. It was missing, so I phoned Terri, who was on her way and would be there in five minutes. When we all met and went inside Terri's home, we found both the mailbox key and Terri's house key on the kitchen counter.

After Bev and I returned home, she stood in the middle of the kitchen and blurted out, "You need a new wife."

"No," I responded, "I love the one I have and we will get through this. Together."

She sat down and just cried and cried, saying over and over, "I can't believe this is happening to me."

At the time I thought I was experiencing my darkest moment

yet. That low point was surpassed, however, by what happened two weeks later.

The final 10 days

On our last trip to Tahoe we talked about my busy schedule – including several days on the road – coming up in November. Our focus would be on the holidays, because I planned to take several days off near Thanksgiving and spend all of December in town, and many of those days would be spent just with her.

On November 1, before leaving for Spokane, Wash., I stopped at home to tell Bev goodbye and to grab my traveling bag. She seemed unusually quiet and sad as we kissed and said our goodbyes. I believe she was already experiencing a great deal of darkness, and my upcoming absence caused her to be fearful.

At a client's capital-campaign Celebration Sunday Brunch on Sunday, November 5, I sat with Ray and Linda Schutte. Ray and Linda had been friends for nearly 40 years, dating back to our Youth for Christ days. Linda has had a series of health complications and is a woman who walks with God in very special ways. She gave me some Scripture to share with Bev when I returned home, and when I spoke with Bev later she was grateful and looked forward to receiving the passages.

My next stop was in Salem, Ore., for lunch with Diane Buchanan, the wife of a close friend and gentleman who I have mentored in the ministry of development. Diane is a nurse with a great deal of experience with people who have Alzheimer's. We discussed appropriate ways for me to interact with Bev and available options as her condition worsened.

That evening, I had an experience that was both frustrating

and embarrassing. My flight from Portland was delayed several hours because of bad weather. When I arrived in Spokane, it was raining hard and I was soaked because of having to walk from the commuter flight to the terminal. About 20 minutes later, I discovered that my luggage was not on the flight. The person in the baggage department calmly informed me that they had simply removed my luggage from the plane "because it was overloaded."

I was furious for two reasons: I was an Alaska Airlines MVP Gold Card holder (their designation for their most-frequent travelers) and I could have simply taken one of my bags on the plane with me – if I had been notified. In addition, had I known about the excess-weight issue, I would have rented a car and driven to Spokane.

The Alaska employee was rude, belligerent and basically indicated he didn't care about my problems. I got to the hotel after midnight, wet, tired, and angry. There I was, with a 7 a.m. client interview the next morning, without my notes or any decent clothes.

The next morning, I called Bev and vented. I realized, later, that my outburst was confusing to her and was probably the worst thing I could have done. I missed the appointment and finally received my baggage late in the morning. I filed complaints with the airline and the agent, but in light of what happened just a few days later, the episode seems very trivial (and has helped me handle subsequent travel delays far better).

"Dad, we are losing Mom."

The next day, Tuesday, November 7, I failed to do something that was a normal part of every travel day: calling Bev to say

"Good morning," tell her I love her, and that I was praying for her day. I don't know why I forgot. It was my final day on the road, with interviews all day and evening, before leaving Spokane for home early the next morning.

About 2:30 p.m., as I was interviewing a couple in their living room, my cell phone rang. Although it was usually turned off during client interviews, I went across the room and answered it. Linda, my assistant, told me Bev had suffered an apparent stroke in a parking lot. A passerby had called 911 and Linda asked me to call Terri immediately for the details.

Terri was nearly hysterical as she told me how firefighters on the scene were taking her mom from her car to Good Samaritan Hospital (a facility that specializes in stroke treatment).

I was stunned and felt incredibly helpless. There I was, 1300 miles away, and my dear wife possibly near death. (Ironically, this was not my first such experience. Seven years earlier, while I was in Pennsylvania, it appeared Bev had suffered a heart attack. I made a frantic trip home and received good news – she had suffered only a hiatial hernia.)

I quickly began to make phone calls, cancelling the rest of my appointments, asking Linda to find a flight home and rushing to my hotel to pack. While there, I e-mailed our prayer request to friends, family, and colleagues who had supported us so faithfully. I told them the agony of not knowing the exact nature of her condition and the aggravation of having to wait three hours to fly out of Spokane to Seattle, where I would have to wait 90 minutes before I could fly to San Jose, arriving at 11 p.m. "God, could Bev be dead by then?" I asked myself. "Why hadn't I called that morning?" Would I ever talk to her again?"

I have flown from Seattle to San Jose probably more than 100 times, a flight of only 1 hour and 45 minutes. But on this evening, it felt like five hours.

The next few hours blurred as I called family, friends and supporters. As often as possible, I tried to reach Terri at the hospital. I had called one of our consulting team, Mike Nauman, as soon as I received the first call, and he had met her at the hospital. She was soon joined by nearly 15 people from church, including two of our pastors.

The trip home was miserable. Not knowing Bev's chances for survival; feeling guilty for being gone; and praying for her recovery - these were the themes that ran through my mind. I was told she had not suffered a stroke but a seizure and was being treated for that condition. She had been placed into an induced coma to hasten recovery, and was expected to get better soon.

When I landed, Mike met me and we rushed to the hospital. I walked through the emergency entrance and was directed to her room. When I entered, I saw no one but Bev, hooked up to many monitors. I called out to her in a fairly loud voice, "Honey, I am here. I am home and I am not going anywhere."

Keith Potter, our senior pastor, arrived shortly after I did, and we talked and prayed together. Bev was expected to come out of the coma the next day. Upon arriving in the waiting room I found Terri, along with many supporters. After talking to some of them and expressing my gratitude, we went to the ICU where the nurse (a wonderful Christian) allowed all of us into Bev's room to pray together.

Driving home I was confused, dazed and afraid. What did all this mean? Would Bev recover? What if she never came out of her coma? Needless to say, I did not sleep well. I asked Trina and Todd to come see their mother ASAP; they both planned on coming up the next day.

I awoke Wednesday with mixed emotions. My original schedule had me leaving the next day for Nashville to chair a Young Life National Capernaum Committee meeting. I called Nick Palermo, the national director, but he already knew the situation and had found another member of the committee to take my place. Another task early that morning was arranging for Ed McDowell to fly to Philadelphia to represent our company at an important training session for a capital-campaign client.

When I arrived at the hospital, Bev was awake and greeted me warmly. She had suffered another seizure during the night and while I was talking to her and the physical therapist, she had two convulsions. Although her body settled down and we resumed our conversation after each occurrence, these episodes were difficult to watch, and my fears mounted again. I was assured that this was normal for someone who had experienced what she had in the previous 24 hours.

Terri arrived and we began to plan for the mid-afternoon arrival of Trina and Todd, and Todd's fiancée. There was plenty to do, including updating our prayer team and calling family and friends.

The five of us had a great time together in Bev's room. She had us laughing as she described her experience before and after she was hospitalized. That evening, the kids and I went out to dinner and discussed the situation.

The doctors said Bev would probably go home on Friday, with medication to control the seizures. Nevertheless, we would need to arrange for in-home care, to assist Terri and me with Bev's care. Trina and Todd decided to go home on Thursday and return on the weekend when she would be at home.

On Thursday morning when we arrived in Bev's room she was surprised to see her family. In fact, she said, "Todd, when did you arrive? It is so nice to see you." We suddenly realized the entire previous day had not registered with her. To say we were saddened would be a big understatement. No one said anything, but there were many anxious looks and glances exchanged.

Later that afternoon, after Trina left to drive home, Todd and I sat in the hospital cafeteria and silently wept as we realized what was happening. Todd said to me, "Dad we are losing Mom." It was a very lonely, fearful moment. We would indeed lose her less than 24 hours later, but in a much different way than we anticipated,

As I lay in bed that night, unable to sleep, I talked with God, telling my heavenly Father, "Dear God, I don't want to say these words but 'Thy will be done.' If Bev has Alzheimer's please take her quickly."

Friday morning, on the way to the hospital, I stopped at the office to get some work done and to prepare for Bev's return home that afternoon. A little after 8 a.m., my office phone rang. It was Bev asking where everyone was. I assured her that Terri and Char were on their way and I would be there soon.

When I arrived, she was alert and ready to go home. The nurse said the doctors were ready to discharge her that afternoon.

Later that morning a member of our church, Sam Sells, stopped by. Sam said the Lord told him to go see Bev Goehner, and so he had come. We had a great conversation and I prayed for him (Sam was facing brain surgery for a benign tumor) and Bev. On his way out he told Bev he would see her in church in a few weeks.

That morning, Bev gave me a little insight into her ordeal in the car on Tuesday. After taking clean laundry to my mom, she made her way to our company office to meet Terri for lunch. Stopping at the

Kentucky Fried Chicken restaurant on Saratoga Avenue, just two and a half blocks from our office, she suffered the seizure after parking the car. The seizure caused her to hit the steering wheel hard enough to cause black and blue bruises to her arms and chest, and nasty cut requiring stitches in her eyebrow.

A passerby noticed Bev slumped over the wheel and opened the car door to help. Bev kept asking her to call Terri, but could not find the phone number. The Good Samaritan called 911 and eventually found a Goehner Group business card and called Terri.

Looking back now, it's so obvious this dear lady gave our family a huge gift - three days with Bev we might not have had and for which we will always be grateful.

All morning, Terri, Bev, Char, and I chatted and enjoyed our time together: At noon, our good friend, Mary Priest, dropped by to talk while Bev ate lunch. Bev's sense of humor was as strong as ever as she removed the chicken from her salad to put into her chicken-noodle soup which, in her words, "Didn't have enough chicken." Mary said she would drop by the house the next day to see how Bev was doing.

About 1 p.m. I excused myself to make a conference call with two of our team about upcoming client visits. I had to go out to my car because my phone was dead and the only charger I had was in the car. As I left, I kissed Bev on the forehead (not on the lips because I felt I was getting a cold and I did not want to expose her) and said I would be back shortly.

Thirty minutes later, Char was pounding on my car window, telling me something had gone wrong and Bev was being treated. Ironically, two incoming calls appeared on my phone but, because I didn't recognize the numbers (one was Char's), I ignored them so I could finish my call before taking Bev home.

I raced into the hospital and frantically made my way to the elevator, only to discover it was going down. I went down one floor and then back up to the third floor. As I reached Bev's room, the door was closing and I saw an oxygen mask on Bev's face. She was bouncing up and down on the bed as the code-blue call sounded and medical staff came from everywhere.

Meanwhile, Terri explained to me that Bev had gone for a walk with the physical therapist while I was on the phone and upon her return could not catch her breath. Nurses applied a cold cloth to her forehead but it did not help, so they called for oxygen and Terri was ordered out of the room. Bev's last words to Terri were "I am going to die."

I began to call everyone I could think of – family, church, friends and the TGG team – and asked them to pray for Bev. Terri, Char and I held each other and hoped against hope that she would be all right. Medical personnel kept going in and out of her room. The longer the episode lasted, the more apparent it was that things were not going well.

By this time, Mike Nauman arrived, along with Kevin Friesen, one of our pastors. At approximately 2:30 p.m., two friends from Simpson University, Dan and Lynn Haskins, arrived with flowers for Bev. They had gotten lost coming to the hospital and theirs was the other call I didn't answer while in my car. Just then, the doctors walked out.

"*We did everything we could.*"

"Doctor, just tell me. Is she dead?"

"*Yes.*"

"What happened?"

"*We are not certain. We want to do an autopsy. We think she suffered a pulmonary embolism but we want to be certain. We are sorry. We worked on her for 30 minutes and got a faint pulse, but nothing more."*

There are no words to describe what I felt at that moment. Terri burst into tears and Kevin Friesen held her in his arms while I stood in shock and disbelief.

How could this happen? Just two hours before, she was laughing and we were looking forward to bringing her going home.

Our God is faithful

A stunning reality

This was the beginning of a surreal time. I could not, would not, accept the reality of what I'd been told. There had to be a mistake. They were talking about someone else…not my precious Bev. She was going home with me. This afternoon! I was going to take care of her, even as she began her journey into Alzheimer's.

Suddenly it hit me: God had answered my prayer. He had taken her home.

The hospital corridor was suddenly full of people. Mary and Tom Priest, Jeff and Becky Davis (neighbors who had come by the night before to pray with Bev), and Greg Davis (another of our pastors) had all rushed to be with us. I called Keith Potter, who was visiting with people at another hospital, and broke the news to him. He rushed to the hospital as well.

My phone rang. It was Todd. I had to tell my son the terrible news. After a moment of silence he began to cry. We were on the phone for some time, grieving together.

Kevin Friesen called Trina and told her the news after asking if someone was with her. She said her son, Carter, was there. She and Carter sat and cried together, and then she had to tell Keaton and Taylor. She called Steen and asked him to come home from work so she and Steen could spend time with our grandsons attempting to deal with the news. She called her aunt, Eldora (my sister) to tell her the bad news. Eldora then called my other sister, Elvera, both of whom are widows.

The events after that hour are blurred. I was on autopilot, giving out phone numbers with instructions for people who should be called, asking Linda (my beloved assistant) to call our Goehner Group team members, and, breaking the news to my sisters. Both Elvera and Eldora are widows and have experienced the death of a spouse.

I began to plan Bev's memorial service after consulting with our pastoral staff. I also called Jene, Bev's sister, who had been praying. She was very quiet at first and then began to weep in disbelief.

About that time, Keith and Kevin grabbed me and said, "Don, we will take care of these details. You go into Bev's room and say goodbye."

My final moments with Bev

Walking into the room I will never forget the sight. My beautiful lady, lying with her mouth open, because of the instrument they had placed in her throat and staring toward the ceiling. I didn't believe it…how could she be dead?

I stood by her bed and wept, talking out loud to God. I didn't ask him why, but just told him what had happened. It was the loneliest moment of my life. For an instant it brought back the moment 47 years earlier when Bev suffered a miscarriage in the latter third of a pregnancy and I was all alone in a hospital 1000 miles from home. But this was now and this was my sweetheart, my wife, my best friend.

Now, what would I do? How could I help my children? All I had were questions, with no answers.

After awhile, Keith asked everyone to come into Bev's room and we gathered around the bed to pray. As I held Bev's face (now turning cold), Keith prayed and thanked God for Bev's life, as well as the fact she was now with the Father in heaven. He prayed for me and our family, and asked God to bring something good out of what appeared to be a tragedy.

I knew I didn't want to be alone, so I invited everyone to my home and Rob Stump (a close friend) quickly organized a dinner party. He brought enough Chinese takeout to feed my entire neighborhood! Mary Priest and Becky Davis were the hostesses that evening, as they would be throughout the initial grieving period.

Kevin drove me to my office so I could send an e-mail to our prayer team. On the way, I called Ardelle, Bev's best friend since their junior-high days. Like the rest of us, Ardelle was shocked and began mourning the loss immediately. I felt helpless to comfort her because I was living in a daze and just barely surviving.

Ardelle Temanson, close friend of Bev Goehner

I was so saddened - in fact, I still am - by Bev's death. She was my best friend. But Don worked through it with dignity. I knew his faith, something he and Bev shared, would be his greatest asset.

Thankfully, Don had a huge group of friends and family to support him. I know my support alone wasn't enough to take care of his grief. People just don't get over the loss of a wife or husband quickly. But Don did find ways to move on, and for that I greatly admire him.

When we arrived at the office, I sat at my computer and composed a very difficult message that began, Bev is with Jesus. The rest of the message appears on Page 191 in the appendix.

A very special evening

When Kevin and I arrived home, Terri, Char and the people who had been at the hospital were getting ready for a dinner.

Three memories from that evening stand out:
- I felt like I was outside my body because the person we were remembering and grieving for was my wife; I just could not grasp the concept.

- My home and cell phone rang often as I talked to caring friends, as well as my children and extended family.
- My feelings were surreal and the cold reality was that I was now a widower.

This special time wasn't without humor. Mary and Becky had warned me earlier, "Beware of widows bringing casseroles."

After saying I wouldn't answer the door, Kevin said, "No, just look through the peephole. If it turns out to be a widow with a casserole, tell her you aren't feeling well, but to please leave the casserole."

At the end of the night, everyone had left except Kevin. He told me he was going to stay with me. He slept on the couch and did not leave my side for the next 24 hours. In retrospect, this was the greatest gift I received following Bev's death. He cooked breakfast, helped me buy a new cell phone, closed out Bev's cell phone service, helped me plan the memorial service and worked with me to prepare for my children's arrival.

Todd arrived on Saturday afternoon, appearing to be near collapse. He had just lost his mom and probably his greatest supporter through his prodigal journey. Steen and Trina arrived on Sunday and we began to plan Bev's service in detail. By this time, Linda had arrived from Cleveland to take charge of the office and help make preparations for the Saturday service.

During that weekend, beginning while I was at the hospital, God put an idea in my mind. I would write Bev a letter (see Page 148 in the appendix), to be read at the beginning of the memorial service on November 18 at our church (Saratoga Federated). I wanted to pay tribute to this woman who had accepted me as I was and had never ceased to love me despite my blemishes and sins.

Honoring Bev Goehner

A sad, surprise announcement

On the Sunday following her mother's death, Terri said she wanted to go to church. Although I was hesitant, I wanted to support her, so we went.

Some people knew of our loss and immediately embraced us, amazed that we had come so soon after Bev's death. During the announcements, Keith mentioned several people who were facing difficult health challenges, including a 15-year-old boy who had come through brain surgery successfully.

He then paused and explained that not everyone is healed, despite our hopes and prayers.

"As many of you know, Bev Goehner was hospitalized this week with a seizure. Just minutes before she was to be released, she suddenly died."

There were gasps and even some cries. He mentioned the upcoming autopsy and, talking about the memorial service on Saturday, urged people to arrive early. *"Don and Bev had many personal and ministry contacts here and across the country, and our sanctuary will be full."*

Following the service, there was a line of people waiting to hug Terri and me, offering condolences and promising to pray for us. I had a chance to share in another's pain that morning, too, as my friend, Dave, told me, "Donna (his wife) has just been diagnosed with Alzheimer's. Don, I knew you would understand."

A service to remember

Throughout the week of November 12 I received calls, e-mails and handwritten sympathy notes and prayer. I was overwhelmed with the amount and depth of support I received. (To read some of these, see Page 180 in the appendix.)

Linda, Terri and the church staff worked on the preparations for the service. I wanted to serve lunch and the church broke precedent, arranging a complete sandwich-and-salad lunch for all the guests.

My children, grandchildren, sisters, brother-in-law, sister-in-law, nieces and nephews began arriving on Friday, the day before the service, and that evening we all gathered at my home for dinner. Linda and Becky rescued us after discovering that the person who prepared the main course had prepared for eight – not the 20 who showed up!

What a night! We sorrowed, we ate, we laughed and we loved each other. One of the highlights was asking Taylor (my middle grandson) to sit on my lap. He was 13 and could have felt very awkward, but he was a good sport about it.

I said, "Taylor, I understand you asked your mom if she thought Grampa would ever remarry."

He grinned, somewhat self consciously as I went on. "I can't imagine that happening, but if it does, you will be the first to know." We all laughed and he grinned even more.

Later that night, I had a wonderful time with Keaton (my oldest grandson) who was staying with me. We talked about life, his grandmother and the upcoming service. I said to him, "Tomorrow, the church will be full and the people who are coming will be honoring your Nama and supporting our family. Keaton, remember they are not coming because she was famous but because she gave her life away for people in the name of Christ."

The next day dawned with me asking God for the strength and courage to get through the service and the day. I prayed that the message of Bev's life and the Scripture shared would communicate clearly to our neighbors (who, to our knowledge, were not Christians).

Keaton and I stopped at one of his favorite restaurants for breakfast and then drove to the church. In the church parking lot I saw my cousin, Del, who lives in the Seattle area, sitting in his rental car. That sight was such a gift! He had driven all this way and his presence at the service gave me a sense of what I would experience all day. God had been, was and would continue to be in charge. Of everything.

As people gathered I was amazed at the efforts people made to be there. They had flown in from the East Coast and the Southwest, as well as from locations up and down the West Coast. I was amazed at the people who had made the effort to come: former Long Beach YFC staff members, current Young Life Capernaum staff members, clients, former members of small groups in various churches, Westmont trustees (20 families were represented), college classmates, neighbors, and others whose lives were changed by Bev.

I tried to meet and greet them all, but Rob Stump, our hospitality lead, escorted me to the family room where everyone was waiting.

One of the greatest tributes Bev and I received that day was the work of the Hospitality Team we had helped establish four years earlier. Members of the parking team wore their green vests, and greeters were everywhere, helping guests find their way to the sanctuary, restrooms, etc. Several people commented later they had "never felt so welcomed arriving at a funeral."

Finally, the moment arrived and our family walked into the sanctuary. It was full, downstairs as well as in the balcony. This was the first memorial service in our newly remodeled sanctuary, where

Bev had been so thrilled less a month earlier when the first worship service was held.

The service was wonderful. Bev had planned it in detail including the songs, the musicians and the Scripture passages. We carried out her plan, with some additions from me. It included our youngest grandson (Carter) reading Scripture, along with three friends. Five people spoke, representing close friends, members of The Goehner Group team, and family.

A DVD presentation of Bev's life began the service, with a soundtrack of music chosen by my sister. Kevin read my letter to Bev (please see Page 148 in the appendix). As I had hoped and prayed, the letter set the stage for the entire service. People cried, laughed and remembered. Several people told me later that they learned more about Bev in those 10 minutes than they had ever known. Keith spoke from I Peter 1:2-7 (Bev's favorite passage in the Bible) and did a marvelous job. Larry Ballenger, a friend of nearly 50 years, prayed for the family and I asked everyone to stay so we could greet them.

I was amazed at the people who had made the effort to come: former Long Beach YFC staff members, current Young Life Capernaum staff members, clients, former members of small groups in various churches, Westmont trustees (20 families were represented), college classmates, neighbors, and others whose lives were changed by Bev.

One neighbor told me, "Bev was the fragrance of Christ in our neighborhood. People went to her to find friendship."

The entire time, Rob Stump was at my side with a sandwich or a bottle of water. What a gift this friend gave me that day!

Dennis Baker, Senior Consultant, The Goehner Group

Don worked through the pain of Bev's death by facing what was going on in his mind and soul, writing, reflecting, and talking about his journey. He sought out seasoned counsel, both professional and peer, and established three or four levels of accountability.

He also had an appropriate amount of interactions and special events with his children and grandsons, each of whom had a special relationship with Bev. Not only did Don not go out and buy himself a gold chain and silk shirt, he protected himself against predator women (except for that one Sunday at church where he was surrounded by 8 to 12 widows and divorcees...).

Following Bev's death I was apprehensive about how he would handle his new life. I feared he would lose himself in work and travel, more travel and more work. There was some of that, but nowhere near as much as I imagined. The positive side of his natural drive to complete tasks and serve others was that his work wasn't left out of the recovery equation – it became a tool for his grieving and healing process.

Our relationship didn't change much after his loss, though I always carved out more time to talk than we scheduled. I listened and occasionally responded. If I was asked a direct question I attempted to answer with grace, mercy and peace.

A final goodbye

On a cold, windy December 27, our family and some special friends gathered at the columbarium at the Monterey City Cemetery to say our final goodbyes to Bev Knowles Goehner.

Prior to the service, I discovered the urn I had purchased was too large and the niche could not be sealed. So, the cemetery worker and I improvised and he simply closed the entire double niche and we made the shift later. Even though we were spared the cold wind during the short service, our time together at the cemetery was much harder than the memorial service. Afterward, Todd said it was the worst day of his life.

Keith did a wonderful job leading this service and several people talked about what they would miss most about Bev. My half-sobbed contribution to the comments was, "I'll miss her prayers." Following the service, we went to Bubba Gump's for dinner and more good conversation. Even on that sorrowful day, we were learning that life moves on.

PART TWO
The Next Chapter in my Journey

On Friday, November 10, 2006, my life changed. Bev, my wife of 48 years, died of a pulmonary embolism. I was instantly ushered into a new journey and, ultimately, a new life.

In the first section of this book, I chronicled Bev's last year and the special experiences she and I enjoyed (without knowing it was to be her last year).

Now, I want to share with you my journey of recovery. There has been pain, loneliness and times of great grief, mingled with times of incredible insight and direction from God's Word, along with the love and support of faithful friends.

Every surviving spouse has their own personal journey and I don't want to pretend that my experience will be the same as someone else's. Nonetheless, I want to share with you some principles I found helpful and, in some cases, literal gifts from God.

I am still working through grief and will be for some time to come, but I am a different person than I was on the afternoon of November 10, 2006. I hope that sharing my journey will be helpful to you.

Reflection and celebration

January 1-6, 2007

As I woke up, I realized this was the first New Year's Day I had experienced without Bev since our marriage in 1959, and the first New Year's without a relationship with her since January 1, 1956 – the day I became a Christian. Wow! Talk about feelings and emotions.

After a disastrous New Year's Eve, I decided to have breakfast with Caryl Taylor, a longtime friend. The conversation was helpful and light, which was exactly what I needed.

Returning home, I packed for my 3 p.m. flight and tried to take care of domestic chores. As Terri drove me to the airport, I felt badly for her; I was going away for a week and she would have ghosts from her past - Dad was traveling again and now Mom was gone, too. Terri has been brave, but I am certain it is lonely for her.

The flight was uneventful and I spoke with Steve Van Atta, a close friend, when I landed. I explained my Christmas gift of money for each family member to buy a gift that would help them remember Bev. He asked a simple question: "What are you buying, Don, which will be your special remembrance?" It began a thought process that would culminate in a decision two days later.

I drove to my cousin Del's and picked up the key for the cottage, as well as instructions for opening and closing, etc. He and I, along with his wife, Elaine, had a very warm and friendly conversation - just what I needed.

From there, I made my way to Wes and Jene's (Bev's sister) and gave them their gifts, which Bev had purchased. It was an emotional time and we all cried a bit. It was apparent that Jene is really suffering. She had agreed to let me pay for counseling and we talked about her beginning in a few weeks. It seemed odd to be at their home without Bev, especially since she was often the life of the party. Her sense of humor and humble spirit were such gifts to all of us.

January 2

I'll soon be headed to Whidbey Island in the San Juan Islands, staying at the Goehner Island Retreat Cottage belonging to Del and Elaine. (When we talked at Bev's memorial service he graciously offered me the opportunity to stay here.)

Wes, Jene and I went to breakfast at Mitzel's before I boarded the ferry to the Island. Prior to departing, I did some grocery shopping for supplies. The ferry ride was nostalgic because I had ridden that ferry with Bev just a few months before, when we stayed on Whidbey Is. during the summer of 2006. Little did I know when we crossed Puget Sound on that late July day that I would never have that experience with her again.

After arriving at Del's place and settling in, I chose to make the first 24 hours a day of silence. I did not talk out loud or with anyone, and did not listen to music. I spent a good deal of time in the Scriptures; these rich moments are reflected in my overall notes regarding the spiritual work I was doing.

First steps

I am looking out of the kitchen window across the Sound at Mukilteo, glancing at the ferry traffic while reading Scripture, praying, and thinking. I spent 30 minutes walking…including climbing Marshall Street to get to the main road.

I prepared six goals I wanted to accomplish during my time here on the Island:

- **Listen** - To the silence…to the Lord…to the water
- **Pray** - Much and often…as the Spirit leads me
- **Read** - Scripture…finish "Hope for the Broken Hearted"…begin book on prayer - reread sections of "A Grace Disguised"
- **Write** - Journal on the computer, as well as by hand in my notebook…and perhaps some work on a book (not likely)
- **Sleep** - When I am tired
- **Walk** – To relax, enjoy the beauty and get some exercise

An ambitious list, to be sure, but even if I accomplish only half of the goals, the time away will have been worth it. I have chosen to live in silence - no music, no TV…just me and God.

My prayer as I began: *Lord, I want to be in the center of your will. I want the Spirit of God to lead my time away. I want to continue the road to healing and I want your guidance on my future. I need to be able to "be on my own" and continue to process Bev's death. Father, you are my only hope and strength. Please meet me in the silence. Amen.*

Listening and reading

God led me back to Psalm 51, which I have read many times. It reminded me again of my sins, my unfaithfulness and my sense that God's justice is part of the consequences of my actions.

I concentrated on Verse 17: *The sacrifices of God are a broken spirit; a broken and contrite heart, O God you will not despise.*

But Verse 16 caught my eye as well. *You (God) do not delight in sacrifice, or I would bring it; you do not take pleasure in burnt offerings.*

That led me to I Samuel 15:22. *To obey is better than sacrifice and to heed is better than the fat of rams.*

That verse directed me to passages throughout the Old and New Testaments, but especially the Old.

- Psalm 40:6-8 (especially Verse 8)
- Matthew 26:39 – *Jesus praying in Gethsemane*
- Isaiah 1:11-15
- Amos 5:24-25
- Micah 6:6-8

Several important questions arose in my mind as a result of my reading:

1. What is God's will in *my* Gethsemane? Matthew 26:39

2. What is right and just for me in my current circumstances? Amos 5:24-25
3. What keeps me from coming to Christ when my burden is heavy? Matt. 11:29
4. What do I bring to the Lord? Micah 6:6
5. How do I really practice Mark 12:33? God, teach me to love you with all I have and to truly love my neighbor…especially those I don't like.

Other thoughts and insights

From Charles Swindoll's calendar, "Grace of Encouragement": *One of the most encouraging things about new years, new weeks, and new days is the word "new"…It is because of the Lord's mercies that we are not consumed, because his compassions fail not. They are new every morning; great is thy faithfulness.* Lamentations 3:22, 23 KJV

Isaiah 66:3: *This is the one I esteem; he who is humble and contrite in spirit.*

Isaiah 61:1-3: *The spirit of the sovereign Lord is upon me, because the Lord has anointed me to preach good news to the poor. He has sent me to bind up the brokenhearted, to proclaim freedom for the captives and release from darkness for the prisoners, to proclaim the year of the Lord's favor and the day of vengeance of our God, to comfort **all who mourn**, and provide for those who grieve in Zion, to bestow on them a crown of beauty instead of ashes, the oil of gladness instead of **mourning**, and a garment of praise instead of a spirit of **despair**. They will be called; oaks of righteousness, a planting of the Lord for the display of his splendor.*

In my Bible I wrote, *Grieving is an act of humility!*

Questions answered
1. What is God's will in my Gethsemane? *To be willing to spend the remainder of my life single. (I have asked for God's will regarding my singleness.) To grieve more deeply than I have and to be restored to ministry in a manner I have never experienced.*
2. What is right and just for me in my present circumstances? *To continue working with those who have not experienced justice and have not been treated right. My faith has to be genuine...not empty words and pious banalities... Child Hope, Rohi and One Stop, organizations working with the poor here and around the world, are steps in the right direction.*
3. What keeps me from coming to Christ when my burden is heavy? *My self-reliance causes me to only want his input on the so-called big things. Statements like "God helps those who help themselves" are not biblical, but reflect a widespread belief about how to approach pain while trying to include God in the equation. I want to experience what it's like to completely place myself in the safe, powerful arms of Jesus.*

It was an intense weekend. Several times I lay on the floor and cried. More than once I sat for long periods of time just pondering. I was committed to do the hard work of grief recovery, and coming to grips with my singleness – a word that has new meaning for me as a widower.

I worked with singles years ago in Southern Calif., but they were young and, in most cases, had never been married. I had been married for nearly 50 years and couldn't remember even being single!

Even as I type these words 90 days later, I can remember the inner turmoil and pain I was experiencing.

During my Whidbey Island retreat I fixed mostly pre-packaged meals – which I discovered later were filled with carbs. (This was prior to receiving my blood-sugar testing device and my initial meeting with a dietician.) I went for a long walk in the afternoon and enjoyed the cold air and the dampness of the surroundings.

A land owner was having trees cut down and a lot prepared just above Del's house on the road. It was a reminder that life continues and change is a constant. As I walked, I wondered what the next few months might hold for me.

The night was surreal. I wanted to dream about Bev but didn't and I finally fell into an exhausted sleep in a very comfortable bed.

LESSONS LEARNED

Many of us struggle from time to time with over-analyzing, re-living the past or asking what-if questions. Going through a life-altering event like I did can cause one to dwell even more on the unknowns, something I knew wasn't healthy.

My friend, Nancy Nelson, gave me a great wake-up call, a question that helped me get my eyes off myself.

"Don't ask, 'Why?' ask, 'Why not me?'"

I found that when I didn't ask "Why," I didn't wonder about all the what-ifs and dwell on the woulda/coulda/shouldas.

What else did I do? For the first two weeks I walked, cried...did anything I could to occupy my mind and avoid not asking what-if questions. For awhile I thought God was punishing me. To my way of thinking, he had ample reason to. After all, I wasn't the husband I should have been; I missed clear signals about Ben's condition, etc.

But, I was determined to not get stuck in the past or in fear. I wanted be a role model for my children and grandchildren. If they were to have positive memories of their mother and grandmother and be able to move beyond her death, my attention needed to be on Bev's wonderful life and legacy, and my own future.

January 3

I awakened early and ended my silence by calling Ed McDowell on his way to the airport to represent The Goehner Group at a client interview in New Jersey. We spoke candidly and openly about my process. Ed agreed to be my accountability partner in this process, partly because of what he'd experienced with his father and father-in-law after the deaths of their spouses.

The highlight of this day was my trip into Langley, Wash., where I took a long walk and then visited the drug store and jewelers Bev and I frequented on each trip to the island. The saleslady listened as I explained I wanted to buy a memory watch and she was thoughtful and sensitive as I looked at several different possibilities. I finally selected two: a Swiss Army watch for work and pleasure, and a Citizen for dress occasions. They were expensive but they have become valued reminders of my special lady.

During the remainder of the day, I worked at my process of grieving and seeking Scriptural promises and guidance. I went to the computer and recorded my discoveries and thoughts. It was a fulfilling day and I walked up the hill again in the late afternoon.

I keep on learning

Never to grieve is never to love. We grieve deeply because we love deeply. Perplexed, but not despairing.

God's glorious grace says: *"Throw guilt and anxiety overboard – draw the anchor – trim the sails – man the rudder – a strong gale (of My Spirit) is coming! Repent, then and turn to God, so that your sins may be wiped out, that times of refreshing may come from the Lord.* Acts 3:19 (NIV).

A helpful Christmas-Eve insight

Steve Jolley, one of the pastors at Steen and Trina's church, quoted Carolyn James, sister-in-law of Kelly James who died on Mount Hood in a climbing accident:

Christmas will come anyway this year, as it always does. From some of the notes Frank and I have received during this difficult time, I'm beginning to think that Christmas is just what grieving people need – not because it distracts from our pain or provides some jolly (but temporary) antidote for depression. Rather it is because sorrow, as one friend put it, "peels back Christmas to the bare essentials" and intensifies our focus on Jesus and why we needed Him to come. Maybe in our sorrow, we have even greater reason to celebrate His coming – for only in Him do we have a solid hope that one day He will wipe away all tears.

I wept as I read this, but she is absolutely correct. Christmas is the beginning of the chain of events which led to the resurrection, my only hope and the only hope for the entire world. Sin brought death, and only Christ's resurrection gives us hope for eternal life - God's plan for humanity. Steve was kind enough to give me the quote and I keep it in my Bible to this day.

During the evening, I spent some time watching the lights of Mukilteo and Everett, as well as the ferry crossing the water. This place has so many memories. This is where my family fished when we were young and the cottage was the cabin my Uncle Chris and Aunt Kleora owned. (Their place always reminded me that their family was much wealthier than mine! They were not arrogant about it and certainly shared, but I always felt like we lived in the "sharecropper's" cabin, and they lived on the house on the hill.)

I slept much better the second night and felt I had fallen into a routine and I would miss this place when I left the next morning.

January 4

I awakened fairly early and got up to finish my retreat. I will be leaving in a few hours and want to finish answering my six questions (to which I will add over time) and reflect on what has transpired during these 48 hours. (Sounds like a TV show…except this is for real!) Continuing the questions I began yesterday (see Page 76):

4. What do I bring to the Lord? According to Micah 6:6 and other Scripture references, I can bring the following:
   - Thanksgiving
   - A broken and contrite heart
   - A broken spirit
   - Music and song = praise
   - Humility
   - A love for justice and mercy
   - A transparent attitude
   - My gifting, my resources, my inner soul
   - Honest attitude regarding my situation
   - My doubt and concerns

5. How do I really put Christ's words in Mark 12:33 into practice? *"To love him with all your heart, with all your understanding and with all your strength, and to love your neighbor as yourself is more important than all burnt offerings and sacrifices."*

Living out this verse requires diligence over a lifetime. Jesus seems to be telling me that my activities, even the religious ones, are meaningless unless I demonstrate my love…toward God and my neighbor. It starts with understanding that God is my Father and he knows what is best for me.

His love is beyond my understanding and his demands are tough, but fair. Love him with all my heart – my emotions and inner soul…with all my understanding – my doubts and questions, as well as the cognitive part of me…and with all my strength – my energy and creative side blended with hard work.

My conclusion: Without God's standard, I could never love my neighbor - I am too preoccupied with me! I can begin practicing by reaching out to my neighbors – near and far – in the manner of the Good Samaritan. That is what I am attempting to do…beginning with my open house and continuing with calls and visits.

I spent some time wrapping up my notes, reading and praying. I was not certain how soon I would have this type of experience again. (Sure enough, I find that three months later I've not had a similar experience.)

What have I learned here on the island?
1. God is sovereign and I will always have questions regarding his will and my response to his call on my life.
2. I had to settle the singleness question before I could be healed.
3. God is sufficient and I can make it …but only with his help and intervention.
4. I have a new reality and new life. It can be good, but it will be different.
5. I did not choose my circumstances, but I get to choose my attitude toward those circumstances.
6. Getting away is a good thing and I need to do more of it.
7. God's word is a treasure.
8. I can't do this on my own…God's spirit is essential in the process.

Ed McDowell, Senior Associate, The Goehner Group

My relationship with Don changed in the months after his loss as we became much closer. We did a lot of life-processing together in our phone conversations. He was blessed with many family members and friends who reached out to him. Their support flowed out of authenticity, genuineness and thoughtfulness.

Early on in the process, Don brought intentionality to his recovery and growth. He sought good counsel, charted a course that made sense for him and stayed true to it.

Grieving is a gift from God, designed to let us explore and experience the depth of love we shared with another who is now gone from us. Our culture does not understand this, but Don came to appreciate and embrace this grieving process through retreats, journaling, conversations, and his own walk with Christ. He had the privilege of reflecting on the life he and Bev lived together in love. That's what grieving is all about - letting grief have enough time to bring about healing.

The trip to Dryden in Central Washington was quite a journey. It began to snow on Snoqualmie Pass and I was grateful for the four-wheel-drive vehicle my assistant, Linda, had rented for me. Those without such equipment were sliding off the road or getting stuck. I got in the left lane behind an 18-wheeler and we made our way to Cle Elum, where the snow lessened. By the time I got to Blewett Pass, it was snowing very lightly and the roads were much better.

My uncle and aunt, Walt and Alvina Goehner; hosted my cousins Keith and Lisa Goehner and Dwight and Carol Goehner for dinner that evening. It was good to be with this family at a very tender time. Alvina was very sensitive to my recent diagnosis of diabetes and prepared some special food for just me. Dwight is diabetic and she has had to deal with this disease over the years.

We had a great evening and I enjoyed bringing them up to date on my journey. This is a special family, one that has always been close to my own family. Walt and my dad were very close and spoke every Sunday up until Dad's death. He and I don't speak that often, but many people think we are brothers, not uncle and nephew.

That night brought another first, as I headed for bed. "Don and Bev's room" was just "Don's room," and I was told it would always be open to me. It just seemed so odd to be there alone, without Bev.

January 5 - An unexpected postscript
Today was the day of the memorial service for Bev in Wenatchee.

My aunt and uncle could not attend the memorial service at our church in California, because Alvina was fighting cancer. I promised I would come to Central Washington and we would watch the DVD of the service together. Over time, plans for the three of us gathering privately grew into a small memorial service for Bev, with family members and high school friends from our central Washington hometowns joining us.

Late that morning, I watched the DVD because I wanted to prepare myself (and make certain the DVD worked). The emotions I felt as I watched are hard to describe. Loneliness, joy, laughter and gratitude for the many memories are just some of what I experienced. I prayed that God would grant me peace and confidence as I moderated the service.

LESSONS LEARNED

I've found that the quality of support widows and widowers get from their church or other group is all over the map. Some congregations have a grief-recovery program that's a true ministry, not just a one-time class or a person in the church who takes in on themselves to reach out to those who've lost a spouse.

Consider recruiting someone to be the grieving person's colleague or mentor. If the match works, it can be an incredible resource. This personal approach acknowledges that everyone grieves differently and a preformatted process just won't work.

As an example of how that help is shown, remember that although grief has no completion date or schedule and you want to be supportive, you may need to confront those in pain if they aren't making progress. Don't let them get stuck in their hurt. Find ways to come close to them and encourage them to look (and live) beyond their grief and loss.

As I prepared to greet people, the first to arrive was Don Voss, a high-school classmate I had not seen in several years. I met his wife and we had some time to talk before others arrived. I had heard that he had become a Mormon and I wanted a chance to share my faith.

We had set up a table with a picture of Bev and a guest book, so friends and family could add their comments about and memories of Bev. I was amazed at the people who came. Gary and Carol Sutton George arrived and greeted me like a long-lost friend. Carol was a member of the Apple Blossom royalty in 1956.

They were followed by Trina Hansen and her husband, the Trina our youngest daughter was named after. Trina spent a good deal of time talking to me and expressed the honor she felt that Bev had chosen to name her daughter after her. I had my picture taken with her and I was able to share how the Lord was sustaining me during this journey.

Nearly 50 people gathered in a small room at the Wenatchee Free Methodist Church where my uncle introduced everyone and we watched the DVD. I then spoke briefly about my journey and retreat. I shared that I was leaning into the pain and was planning to live a full life, including working for five more years. Rod Brown, a pastor friend, prayed a wonderful prayer of dedication. Don Voss was overwhelmed at my response to the loss of Bev, and told me how proud he was of me.

It was a great evening and a chance to share our faith with people who are unchurched. I had a chance to speak to Swede Weedman, my cousin, who looked like he had been hit by a truck. His wife, Angie died in September and it was apparent he does not have the support I do. I later wrote to him and sent him Jerry Sitser's book, "A Grace Disguised: How the Soul Grows through Loss." (For a list of the other books on grief that helped me, see Page 205 in the appendix.)

One of my high-school classmates told me he could not have done what I had done. My response was simple: "Without Christ, neither could I. He is getting me through this, day by day."

Journal to Bev

(Writing to Bev in my journal was an idea I got from Mike Sampley, a marriage and family therapist and a staff member at Laurelglen Bible Church in Bakersfield.)

February 18, 2007

Dear Bev,

It's been three months since God called you home. There have been many changes and challenges for me, as well as routines which remain unchanged.

I am on a plane to Portland and then will head to Spokane on Sunday morning. The trip is an all-too-painful reminder of the frustrations you felt with my schedule. This time I not only agreed to give a report to a client without checking my calendar, but I then discovered that this is President's Day weekend. One thing led to another and now I am basically working this entire weekend.

I'm not happy about my schedule and won't repeat this mistake next year. As Terri drove me to the airport and discovered that she has tomorrow off and I am working. Her comment was, "Dad, that's not fair."

But I am so happy you have been delivered from the frustrations you felt about my schedule and my inability to say no to people's requests for my time.

Sweetheart, Ed McDowell's words at your memorial service are ringing in my ears: "Bev, it is an unusual woman who shares her husband with the world."

Honey, that is exactly what you did – you shared me with everyone and paid a high price. I am most sad about the fact you didn't live to experience our dream of us spending lazy mornings together and having a retirement life as we grew old together.

Every day I become more aware of what a gift you were to me and the amount of sacrifice you made for me, our children, and our grandchildren.

You are not here and we are all grieving. Thankfully, our grieving is not like some, because we have hope. Paul, writing to the Thessalonians in Chapter 4, Verses 13 and 14, stressed *"We do not want you to be ignorant about those who fall asleep, or to grieve like the rest of men, who have no hope. We believe that Jesus died and rose again and so we believe that God will bring with Jesus those who have fallen asleep with him."* That hope was evident just now as I prayed, thanking God that I am one day closer to seeing you again. I have never been more anxious for the return of Christ!

You would be so proud of Todd as he blossoms and flourishes in several areas. He has been serving as interim director at his agency and is now working on a special project in Santa Paula.

Todd Goehner, Don and Bev's son

As much as it was helpful to talk with others about the loss of my mom, I had to do a lot of the grief work on my own. Not only did we all have our own personal relationships with Mom, but because I was her only son I didn't go through much of the process with my sisters.

I think the bottom line was my mom and I had been very close and suddenly I didn't have her anymore. So, I needed to face the pain I felt and my desire to move forward. Plus, I believed that one way I could honor my mom was by getting healthy and not getting stuck. That's what she would want for me and my family members.

As I worked my way toward healing, I gained valuable perspectives from time spent with a therapist. I also discovered that some of my relationships needed to change - even end - so I could focus on dealing w/ my mother's death.

I've known so many people who were bitter about some past loss and I didn't want to be like that. I decided I would do whatever I had to do to move beyond my pain. Twenty years from now I want to know I've dealt with things in healthy ways.

It's all about making the grief real for yourself, exposing the pain, getting to the healing. Pain really is the doorway to healing. Like they say in many 12-step programs, "The only way out (of the hurt) is through (it)."

Todd appears to be processing your death better than either of the girls. Is it possible that your death forced him to become the man he was meant to be?

Trina appears to be struggling. I hope you know this and can speak to the Father about it. I am trying to talk to her as much as possible, but I can never replace you. Trina misses your calls and the chance to tell you about your grandsons. As you know, being a mom is a full-time job. Trina is multitalented and seems to be on the move 24/7. She reminds me so much of you.

The boys are growing and changing. Taylor is an all-star in soccer and having a good basketball season. He is doing his best in school and I think Trina is realizing that academics are not his passion. He is a good student and in most families would be considered excellent. Unfortunately, he's sandwiched between his academic-all-star brothers.

Keaton is behaving like a teenager but still very courteous. We have had some good telephone conversations. I am planning to ask Trina to allow me to take him to the East Coast and, in particular, Washington D.C., for a vacation with his grandpa. In addition, he is interested in working at Warm Beach Camp during the summer of 2008, and I am going to help him pursue that opportunity.

Carter continues to be delightful. He has developed into quite an athlete! He loves water polo and plays a mean game of basketball. He won the 5th-grade spelling bee and competed for the school championship. He did not win and may have felt like he failed because Keaton won when he was a 5th grader.

Steen is beginning to flourish in his new position at Elings Park. Shortly after you died, a staff member led a revolt against Steen's leadership, but the board of directors squashed it. Since then, all but one of the problem employees has left and he is beginning to develop his own staff.

He is also working for The Goehner Group and I am discovering how talented he is. Honey, Steen has been a rock throughout this transition. He calls me regularly and is such an encouragement. We were blessed when he joined our family!

That brings me to Terri. It is a difficult time for her and me. She is grieving the loss of her mom and her grief has resulted in some sensitive times for both of us. (I'm not sure how Heaven works, but if possible, would you speak to the Father about this - on behalf of all of us?) She is trying hard to be strong for me and I think, at times, she could spend more time working through her grief. She works hard at the office and has been an encouragement to me as I have learned to cook.

Honey, I miss you terribly and I am working hard to adjust. One of my new challenges, diabetes, is causing me to change my lifestyle. Although I've lost at least 15 pounds, it is a challenge to do this without you because I know you would have cooked accordingly and worked hard to buy the things I need. I am learning and think you would be proud of how I am managing. But it is really, really hard without my life partner.

I have done some things to make life more upbeat. I held an open house for 20 neighbors in January. Many came and Sean, Wendy and their children stayed most of the afternoon. Natacha and Coral stayed the entire time and Jeff Davis was able to talk to her about being a single parent.

In preparation for that event, your friend, David, remarked, "Bev was the fragrance of Christ in this neighborhood." Wow! What an impact you had in your own quiet, grace-filled and hospitable way.

You demonstrated the love of Christ in so many ways – hospitality, prayer and the many open-houses you hosted when we lived in Ventura. And, your special touches at Christmas. Everyone loved your applesauce cakes!

This week I invited people to join Terri and me on Valentines evening. Seven of us had dinner together and enjoyed an evening of laughter and conversation. It helped make the day and evening bearable. I would have preferred a quiet dinner with you but I am trying to adjust to my new life.

As time passes, I am more aware of the gift you were to me and even if I remarry, it won't be the same. You were the love of my life and I miss you so much that tears come to my eyes as I type these words. I find that grieving is hard work and I am glad I am the one going through this rather than you. I believe grief would have been a very difficult journey for you, especially given some of your health issues. I think it is easier for me to adjust to the household duties than it would have been for you to adjust to financial management.

Sweetheart, I can't wish you a good day because where you are there are no days. Thankfully, you are experiencing what God intended for us all. I just am so glad to express my feelings and tell you again I love you, miss you and will never forget you.

Don

Second journal to Bev

August 2007

Dear Bev,

I just reread my journal from February 18, which I wrote at the suggestion of a counselor. I can't believe five months have passed.

I am sitting at the dining table in Del and Elaine's cottage on Whidbey Island. They have allowed me (for the second time in six months) to use it. The first time was in January when I came here to mourn you and ask God to give me the strength to go on. I sure need the Lord's comfort and help.

I miss our phone conversations. Sometimes I think to myself, "I need to tell Bev about this," but then I realize I can't. My journals, I hope, serve as a kind of substitute for the real thing. God has been my sufficiency, but it has been very difficult and, at times, seems impossible.

This week in particular will be difficult because I am going to two of our favorite places: The Wedgewood Hotel in Vancouver and the Anderson house in Roberts Creek. Yes, Janet's house without a shower!

Both of these were favorites of ours and I have great memories of our times together at each location. I feel it is important for me to visit them in order to increase my healing. I know I will cry a great deal this week as I remember you and our wonderful life together.

I am so glad we traveled as much as we did and experienced all of the adventures together. I remember our visit two years ago to Young Life's Malibu Camp, arriving on the Young Life boat. It was an all-day experience we both enjoyed immensely.

Janet will meet me on Wednesday morning at her home and cook me breakfast before she heads backs to her home in Vancouver. What a gift she has given us over the years. One of her gifts to me has been a book, "Pilgrim Prayers," that has been very helpful.

Honey, you can't believe how incredible the Body of Christ has been to me during the past nearly nine months. I would exchange all of that in a heartbeat if I could spend some time in conversation with you and have the joy of holding you in my arms. The intimate conversations and snuggling are what I miss the most.

A lot has transpired since I last wrote and I will try to summarize my life and our family journey.

Keaton and I did make the trip to Washington D.C. We spent 11 days together, beginning in Boston and working our way south to Williamsburg and then back to Washington. (The route was very similar to the trip we made with Todd and Trina in 1979.) You would be so proud of him. He is a very good looking and polite young man. He made an incredible impression on every adult he met. In fact, Mark Harmon (Pam's husband and our guide in D.C.) noted that he could count on the fingers of one hand teenagers of Keaton's caliber.

We had an incredible time, but I thought of you several times and wished you could have joined us. Terri reminded me, however, that your health would have probably prevented it. It was the dream trip you and I envisioned when we discussed it about a year ago.

Keaton has his driving permit and he is going to be a good driver. I rode with him in the "Namamobile" on June 23 when we celebrated my Father's Day. Oh, yes…I gave your car to the Hudson boys on Easter. They had to complete a scavenger hunt before finding it in the garage! Steen is driving it and Keaton will drive the Camry that Steen had been driving. It seems to be working out for everyone;

I'm so glad the car and its personalized license plates are staying in the family.

Taylor broke another bone in May. This time it was his foot, while skateboarding. That injury ended his basketball and soccer all-star seasons. He is becoming gun shy about his injuries. He did a marvelous job academically this year and will be an eighth grader this fall. That means he will have a graduation next June. I will be there and I know you will be too…in spirit! Taylor is doing Junior Lifeguards this summer, but I am not sure how much he really enjoys it. (His mother definitely influenced the decision.)

That brings me to Carter. He is at Forest Home this week (Keaton and Taylor went earlier this summer) and is having a wonderful summer between Junior Lifeguards and water polo. The two sports go hand in hand and he is one tough little dude. Honey, he looks just like you and behaves like a mixture of you and me. I treasure him because he is a constant reminder of you!

Trina seems to be doing better but she really misses her mother. We are all amazed at how much she looks like you and lives life in a similar manner. Todd and Terri are always commenting about how much like you she is. Of all three, I think she misses you most, but her hectic lifestyle doesn't leave much time to mourn. She is working for Steen's organization part-time and doing a marvelous job. Sweetie, please intervene with the Father on her behalf.

Steen has revolutionized Elings Park and seems to be enjoying his new position. He is incredibly patient with Trina (as she is with him) and is doing a great job for The Goehner Group. I really think he will take over the company some day.

Trina Hudson, Don and Bev's daughter

Dad's grieving process seemed natural and real. Mom was dead and that's how we talked about it. He was able to honor her, her life and her memory, yet move forward in appropriate ways. He slowly got rid of her things and made the house look more masculine, as he began his life as a widower.

I trust my dad and wasn't concerned about how he would handle things following Mom's death. I knew he would be sad and miss her, but I also knew he would survive, adjust, and manage.

As for my own feelings of loss, the hardest part was not being able to talk with her. I just wanted (and still want) to pick up the phone and tell her things, or ask her to pray with me about things, or just laugh with her about life, and kids, and being a mom. All of us, Dad and the kids, appreciated phone calls, and people checking in on us. It was also good to talk about Mom, to remember her and how much fun she was.

My dad and I probably talked more after Mom died. I checked in with him, just to see how he was doing. I was proud that he learned how to cook and do his laundry!

We all grieve in different ways, but going forward is the important part. Death is permanent and we have no control over it - we can only control our responses to it. Someone whose parent has died needs to find ways to work through it, to talk with people they trust. That's healthy. Being able to talk about death, and the pain and loss you've experienced, is a vital part of the healing process.

Terri is doing better than I expected. She and I attended a grief-recovery class at SFC and she has begun a small group of women who are meeting every Monday evening during the summer. In addition, she has gone into her Goehner-family leadership mode:
- She's the chairwoman for the women's retreat next March at Mission Springs (This will be her third and last time to lead but she feels that they have changed the emphasis and it will never go back to what it used to be.)
- She is directing the Hospitality Center because both Rob and Jim have had to step away
- She will chair the task force that determines the future of women's ministry at SFC

She is doing her best to keep your memory alive through her plants and also by watering mine.

Todd is the miracle story. He continues to blossom and is now in a new role with LSS. He has four offices: Westlake, Thousand Oaks, Oxnard and Santa Paula. His picture will be in the Ventura County Star and he received a commendation from the city of Santa Paula for his work with the relief efforts for migrant workers. He and Char are not engaged anymore and I don't know what the future holds. He and I talk several times a week and he joined Terri and me for four days at Jim Slevcove's home at Bass Lake over the Memorial Day weekend.

LESSONS LEARNED

My children are all different and, naturally, needed different things after their mom's death. Bev influenced their lives greatly and I'm still learning to be sensitive.

Todd appeared to be the most vulnerable of the three, but turned out to be strongest. He needed to vent and it was often to his dad. We're close and we've been through a lot of grieving together. Terri and I have been close for years – we work in the same office and live very near one another – but her mom's death caused her to build a new circle of friends. Trina is married and has a full family life of her own. I have tried to be available and have gotten as involved as I could in her sons' lives. (She has given me a great gift – three wonderful grandsons and she is a great mom!) Trying, I guess if I'm honest, to do a little double duty as grandpa and grandma.

Finally, a few words about me. I am not certain you would recognize me. I have lost more than 30 pounds since you went to be with the Lord. I have my diabetes under control through diet and exercise. I exercise rigorously and it is becoming a way of life. Honey, I am proving that I can live on my own:

- I do my own laundry and ironing
- I am learning to cook and entertain on a regular basis

- I will be going to a cooking class with Sue Potter this fall
- I had a new deck built and it is just what you wanted!
- I am beginning to change out the house, starting with new couches (Todd and Trina are getting the old ones)
- I am shopping, running errands, etc.

I am even taking 27 days of vacation this summer. You are probably asking the Lord: "Why didn't he do that when I was alive?" I don't know the answer, Bev, but I do know I am working hard to have boundaries and a more balanced life. You know that is hard for me because I am so driven.

Entertaining in our home has been one of those steps forward, spending time with people who are our friends, even though sometimes it is hard because I am single. I am spending time with some women in what I hope are healthy, friendship relationships. It feels very odd.

I am setting boundaries with Terri so she will build a new life with her own friends, and not just continue spending time with only you and me.

There is much more I could tell you but I will do so in my next communication. Until then, I love you, miss you and will never forget you.

Love,

Don

New Years' reflections

January 1-5, 2008

I arrived on Whidbey Island about noon on New Year's Day and departed at noon on January 5. The visit was scheduled to be shorter but I decided on New Year's night to cancel my trip to the Wenatchee Valley because of the accumulated snow and forecast for heavy storms. The next morning, I called Walt and he was in total agreement. In fact, he had been thinking about calling me.

My time was interrupted once with a trip to Everett for a Warm Beach capital-campaign meeting on Friday morning. I left at 5:30 a.m. and returned at noon. Apart from that trip, I spent all my time at the cottage, except for trips to Langley to walk, have one breakfast and one dinner. I did no shopping and did not do any driving as I did last summer.

Instead, I stayed close to the cottage and spent time writing in my 2006 and 2007 journals; reading; studying the Bible; and prayer. I relaxed and even watched a couple hours of TV. (It was soon apparent why I don't have a TV at home - little of the programming has any value.)

Although there were big differences between my retreats this year and last (which I'll describe later), this was a wonderful way to start a new year. I am deeply grateful for Del and Elaine for making this cottage available.

What a difference a year makes!

I am different today because I am at a different place in my journey to healing and recovery. One year ago, I remember lying on the floor and crying because I missed Bev so much and I felt so alone.

This year, I felt sadness but it was of a different nature. I am sad because we were denied the joy of growing old together and she will miss many great events in the life of our family.

A year ago, I felt isolated and my only calls were to people like Joan Newlon (who was recovering from a near-fatal illness) and Janet Anderson (who had called to offer spiritual counsel). I spent 24 hours in silence in 2007 (a very deliberate decision on my part), time that was enormously healing. This year I was in constant contact with people and even called my office and dealt with some business issues.

As I lay on the couch praying on Thursday, I realized I had made great progress and so I read my 2007 goals which I developed while here on the Island. I was amazed at how many goals had been accomplished and how many were at least partially completed. When I wrote the goals in early 2007 I was living day to day and, sometimes, only a half day at a time. There was little or no basis for the goals but because I am a goal-oriented person, I included them in my 2008 personal plan (something I try to do each year).

Now, one year later, there are actually very few on which I have made no progress; in some cases the goals are no longer valid. I realize how far I have come and how God has proven faithful.

To help me move beyond surviving to thriving, I reviewed each goal and noted my progress in red. This also helps me establish goals for 2008, which I intend to do tomorrow before I start my work year on Monday.

One year ago I was trying to discover if I could live the remainder of my life alone, aware that Caryl Taylor could become a person in whom I'd be interested. My goal and commitment was to maintain a friendship while transitioning to my new "normal." So many widowers rebound from losing their wives to marrying; I was determined not to be among them.

One year later, Caryl and I are dating and we genuinely love each other. It has been a marvelous journey and I feel she is a gift of God to me. I still don't know if I will remarry and that is just fine. In the past year, I have proved I can live alone…and even enjoy it!

Caryl Taylor Goehner, Don's wife

> Don processed Bev's death by accepting - and even embracing - his pain. He did not run from it or try to minimize it, but simply faced it head on, relying on the Lord to get him through it. He has actually grown closer to the Lord throughout the whole process.
>
> At first, I wasn't sure how he would handle Bev's death, but I wasn't concerned that he'd remain broken. There were times he'd call, almost in tears over Bev or her death. I just listened. I hurt for him and wanted to help, but didn't give him advice or platitudes.
>
> I think Don appreciated those family members and friends who reached out to him by simply telling him they'd be there whenever he needed them. And, they backed up their offer by really meaning it! Phone calls, telling him they were praying for him, allowing him to grieve in his own way without telling him what to do – all these were gifts of incredible value to Don and his healing process.

Learning to go forward after the loss of your spouse is hard, but close friends and family who are available are a huge blessing. Nothing helps someone more than hearing, "I've been where you are and I know how much it hurts."

—⚘—

What hasn't changed

I still need time away and know it's hard work for me to schedule the necessary downtime. I am so driven that I find it difficult to simply relax. Sometimes I feel guilty when I do something as innocent as lying on the couch. It is sad to realize that my life is has become so programmed I do not have (or take?) time for me.

Despite this realization, I did better in 2007 in terms of getting away to do fun things. From April to August, I made sure to go somewhere every month; that was very regenerating. I took the longest vacation in my life that summer. I violated my rule in September and October, however, and was worn out by the time I reached the first anniversary of Bev's death on November 10. I got back on schedule during November, December and January 2008, and am working hard to stay on track with regular breaks in 2008.

I want to be God's man and this time away for me was another reminder of how the Lord gets crowded out of my busy life. Intentionally seeking and being with God is work, and I need to approach it with the same intensity I do my professional work. Time with the Lord is the source of my strength.

Being a man of God has taken on new meaning. It means reading Scripture; pursuing intense times of prayer and silence before God; and worshipping with God's people. It also means taking action.

I want to serve others based on the love Christ has spread abroad in my heart as I try to live out Jesus' instruction in Matthew 25 to minister to the "least of these."

I love this place in the San Juan Islands. Whidbey Island is quiet, quaint and peaceful. I love the view of Puget Sound and the ferries passing back and forth between Clinton and Mukilteo, as well as to and from the town of Langley. This particular site, south of the ferry dock, is a throwback to my youth and the great memories I have of fishing on Whidbey and staying in cabins on this very property.

What are my takeaways this year?

- History does not repeat itself. Each retreat is different because I have different needs at different times in my life
- The "Valley of Vision" book of prayers by Arthur Bennett is an invaluable guide to devotional thinking and prayer. Some quotes from the book that spoke especially to me during this retreat:
    - "That my wound of secret godlessness might be cured." I have struggled in this area and this is truly my prayer. God, I want to be in private what I am in public. Forgive me when I have not been.
    - "Let me never forget that heinousness of sin lies not so much in the nature of the sin committed, as in the greatness of the Person sinned against."
    - "What I now have in Christ is mine in part, but shortly I shall have it perfectly in heaven."
- Writing is therapeutic. Whether it is writing daily in my journal or writing a potential book draft, it is a way to clear my mind, cleanse my soul and feel creative. This has been

the highlight of this retreat. I have made great progress on my book, "*Ten Months and Ten Days: A Celebration of Bev Goehner's Life,*" and completed my 2007 journal. It was really hard work, but extremely healing.
- It's a good thing to set goals and it's important to review at the end of the year. As a goal-oriented person, I need goals against which I can measure my progress. I am also a list person, checking off completed tasks and reviewing progress. A quarterly review is important, something I did not do in 2007. It's one of my 2008 goals.
- I need a theme passage of Scripture for 2008, especially after finding the value of such passages during 2007. I found it in one of my favorite sections of Scripture, Romans 12:9-21: "*Love must be sincere. Hate what is evil; cling to what is good. Be devoted to one another in brotherly love. Honor one another above yourselves. Never be lacking in zeal, but keep your spiritual fervor, serving the Lord. Be joyful in hope, patient in affliction, faithful in prayer. Share with God's people who are in need. Practice hospitality. Bless those who persecute you; bless and do not curse. Rejoice with those who rejoice; mourn with those who mourn. Live in harmony with one another. Do not be proud, but be willing to associate with people of low position. Do not be conceited. Do not repay anyone evil for evil. Be careful to do what is right in the eyes of everybody. If it is possible, as far as it depends on you, live at peace with everyone. Do not take revenge, my friends, but leave room for God's wrath, for it is written: "It is mine to avenge; I will repay," says the Lord. On the contrary: "If your enemy is hungry, feed him; if he is thirsty, give him something*

to drink. In doing this, you will heap burning coals on his head." Do not be overcome by evil, but overcome evil with good."

This Scripture is practical and measurable, two important components of my spiritual journey.

Dear Lord,

As I depart this island, may I leave different than I came. May people see that I have been with Jesus. May I walk forward in the light of your word with the confidence that you love me and want the best for me. May Job 13:11-12 become my reality: "*My feet have closely followed his steps; I have kept to his way without turning aside. I have not departed from the commands of his lips; I have treasured the words of his mouth more than my daily bread.*"

Amen!!

Learning to walk in - and through - grief

A "kept" husband

Friends tease me about how Bev and I differed on domestic and family matters, saying she basically raised me. From her earliest years as a child, she had always wanted to be married and have children. Married at 19 ½, we were parents before our 22nd birthdays. She was an early riser and extremely motivated. She worked during my last two years of college and Terri, our oldest, was born just two months after I completed my bachelor's degree.

Bev was the consummate mother and wife, handling all the house duties like cooking, shopping, laundry, and much more. She was a Proverbs-31 woman before the term became popular.

I, on the other hand, was a procrastinator who got by on verbal skills and my passion for relationships with people. Although I was not born an early riser, I became one as I developed into a workaholic who was away from the home for meetings many evenings of the week, and traveled extensively for the organizations with which I worked. Furthermore, I had a creative mind that was not practical or prudent.

Bev supported me in every way and I simply did not pay much attention to the "home front" of our marriage. On November 10, 2006, in a matter of minutes, that changed completely. I went from a marriage partnership and having a lifetime helpmate to being alone. Today, as I write about my experience, I realize how much I have changed from those early years.

My brother-in-law, Wes, remarked to Jene, Bev's sister, after Bev's memorial service, "What is Don going to do? He can't even boil water."

Sadly, his comment wasn't far from the truth. I needed to start learning how to take care of a household and take on duties and responsibilities that were foreign to me. It's been challenging, but the experience has been invaluable to my healing and growth. I have gone from being a kept husband to a widower who has learned to survive and even thrive. Becoming confident as a manager of my home is just one way I've changed.

Leaning into the pain

Following Bev's sudden death, a group of friends gathered at our home for dinner and conversation.

That evening, Kevin Friesen gave me the first of many valuable gifts. He stayed with me for 36 hours, cooking me breakfast, helping me buy a new cell phone, and starting to plan Bev's memorial service with me. He was there when my children from Southern Calif. arrived. His presence comforted and strengthened me immensely.

But the most important thing Kevin did was to give me a mission statement for my grief. He reminded me that Keith Potter, my pastor, had preached a sermon a few months earlier on pain. Keith had identified three possible responses to the pain we all inevitably experience in our lives:

1. **Deny it exists** – but you will never get to the core of your issues, and your friends will realize you are in denial and nowhere near the inner healing you need.
2. **Try to avoid pain** – but temporary success in dodging hurts will lead to increasingly severe pain without any tools to live through it.
3. **Lean into the pain** - much like a downhill skier attacking the slope or a driver steering a car in the direction of the skid.

This pathway - leaning into the pain - is the one I chose and I have never regretted my decision.

Kevin Friesen, one of Don and Bev's former pastors

Don was as intentional about grieving as anything else I've seen him do. His choices about how, when and where to grieve were consistent with how he lives. What was more important than anything is that he made grieving a central part of his life. He was deliberate about seeking health and healing by grieving Bev in every way possible. He made the time and space in his life for grief. He planned for it, even spent money to put himself in opportune settings to grieve. Don had the wisdom and courage to show up and grieve.

I was concerned that grieving and transitioning would be just another project for Don. He's so good at going after something and getting it done, but something like grief can't be treated like a task on a to-do list. Grief needs to accomplish its purpose in its own way and time.

Don and I became much closer after his loss. We were two men who never imagined we'd be single, but were (albeit for totally different reasons). We both had previously unavailable time and were motivated to nurture a mature friendship where we didn't have to worry about bringing the other person along or ministering to them. The only reason I was available and able to love and encourage Don was because of my own story of loss and grief.

Family members and friends reached out to Don after his wife died by entering into the normalcy of his everyday life. They helped him find a new normal, one that worked for him and worked without Bev. It was familiar people in familiar places, such as having dinner with him at his house.

My advice to people who want to love and support a grieving parent, friend or colleague involves three actions:

Show up – There's nothing more important than simply being there for them.

Listen – Encourage them to talk (while you listen). Your presence in their life is way more important than your opinion.

Support their grieving process – If you must say something, offer words and thoughts that encourage your friend to fully embrace their grief.

This is not a season that can be short-changed. Whatever doesn't get grieved now will find its way out later - often in a much more disruptive manner. Don't try and help them get over it, help them get through it.

Choose your attitude

Kevin was not the only person who gave me practical advice. Longtime friends Jim and Nancy Jensen had been in a small group with us for several years while we lived in Southern Calif. Jim, Nancy and I had attended Westmont College at the same time. Nancy became a widow in 1996 when Jim died quite suddenly of esophageal cancer.

Nancy told me, "Don, you can't choose your circumstances but you can choose your attitude."

I began to speak that truth to myself nearly every day. I was determined to work through my grief but I sometimes found myself just overwhelmed, ready to give up. Nancy's words kept ringing in my head, "…you can choose your attitude."

I have been open with people during my grieving process, inviting them into my thoughts and feelings – hopefully without being maudlin or self-pitying. I e-mailed my supporters regularly. I asked those who had prayed for Bev's recovery to pray for a different kind of recovery – this time, for me. I called friends who had given me permission to contact them and talked about my struggles and victories. I sought out people who were further along the grief and recovery journey than me, and I read book after book.

One way I controlled my attitude was my approach to the length of time since Bev's death. Rather than dwelling on the days, weeks and months I had been alone, I worked hard to see myself as one day closer to being with her again.

I was committed to being positive and to getting healthy. I had watched others become isolated, bitter and angry, and then retreat into a shell. I wanted to prove God was faithful, while overcoming the fears that gnawed at me just below the surface.

I understand this has been a journey of personal and spiritual growth, one I would not have wanted to miss because it's made me a different person. Yes, I would have liked to have selected a path of my own choosing, but, I wasn't controlling the circumstances. What I did have control over, however, was my reaction to my circumstances. I learned to control my attitude instead of letting my circumstances control me.

A friend speaks truth into my life and journey
I met Tom Nelson, a close friend for more than 30 years, when I worked at Azusa Pacific University in the '70s. He is a straight-shooter, never bashful about expressing his opinion or giving advice. When we met for the first time, his opening questions were, "What are you doing here? And, do I need to bother to get to know you or are you just a short-timer?" Like I said, with Tom I always knew where he – and I – stood!

We became great friends and I walked with him throughout a difficult divorce. We did lots of things together as couples, such as weekend trips and vacations. We laughed together, cried together and shared our lives including some years in a small group. Tom joined the Westmont board of trustees a few years after me and together we have served that institution for more than two decades each.

He and Bev had a special relationship. Perhaps it was because, like him, she could be direct and blunt! When Tom began his career as a financial planner, we were among the first couples he visited. After talking with us about the products and services he thought best for us, Bev asked, "Well, Nelson, is this how you treat all your friends? You just try to get their money?" Tom never forgot that moment and from then on they had a unique relationship.

Shortly after Bev died, Tom drove to Northern Calif. to visit me. He looked me in the eye and said, "Goehner, remember you're starting a journey. So don't think about getting married or even having a serious relationship until you do three things:

- Learn to do your own laundry. It's pathetic that you don't know how.
- Learn how to cook and enjoy it. Have guests over.
- Enjoy singleness for at least three years.

Tom was right and I am so fortunate to have a friend like him. Those three points became a key to my recovery plan.

My plan

Those who know me well will not be surprised at how two dominant characteristics in my personality - planning and competiveness - played a large role in my journey. First, I admit I don't like to lose and I am competitive at everything, including board games. Tell me I can't do something and I am bound and determined to not just do it but succeed at it.

Early on, I was determined that I would not let grief win the battle for my attitude. I was committed to grieving and facing it head on, while not allowing it to dominate me.

Second, I am a planner. I'm usually prepared for everything, from my daily schedule to vacations to having dinner with friends. I never wonder what I'm trying to accomplish.

My plan for dealing with and moving beyond grief had the following action steps:

- Read lots of books about grief
- Spend time reading Scripture, seeking God's peace and direction

- Make time for personal retreats
- Concentrate on being a good father and grandparent
- Keep Bev's memory alive
- Learn to accept the new normal and the person I'm becoming.

I soon discovered that my new normal simply meant nothing would ever be the same again, not for me, not for my family, indeed, not even for our nation and world.

Annual retreats

A few weeks after Bev died, I realized in order to carry out my plan I needed to get away and spend time alone. I had often considered taking a personal retreat, but except for one or two occasions early in my ministry, had never taken the time to get away and be alone with God.

I contacted my cousin, Del, who owns a wonderful little cottage on Whidbey Island in the state of Washington. This familiar spot is where my family went salmon fishing when I was a child. To call it a resort is a stretch because we stayed in fairly primitive cabins, but it still held fond memories for me. My uncle, Chris, purchased a larger cabin on a ridge above the cabins in which we stayed. Del later turned it into a very nice retreat cottage. Del agreed to let me stay there when I began my journey through grief on January 2, 2007.

For the next three days I read, prayed and wrote. Some of that time was spent on the floor of the living room weeping and asking God to give me the strength and courage to make it through. My first 24 hours were spent in complete silence. (I was responding to a challenge I received at a Brendan Manning seminar a year or so earlier. It was also something I had done while serving with Youth for Christ in the '60s and '70s.)

The days spent in what became a sacred place was the beginning of my journey to health. In my writing, I was very honest and cried out to God for help and strength. When it felt like my world had ended I prayed fervently for peace. I asked God for a special measure of courage to face life as a widower and the father of three adult children who adored their mother.

> ### LESSONS LEARNED
>
> *I've been asked when and how I started thinking of myself as a widower or a single man. I don't think I ever saw myself as single. I remember the first time I had to fill out a form and check the "Widower" box. That was hard because I realized I was no longer married, not because I thought of myself as being single. In some ways, being a widower was almost a badge of honor. It showed I had had this wonderful person in my life - Bev.*
>
> *The key to releasing myself to begin a relationship with Caryl Taylor (and a possible future with her) was, surprisingly, celebrating my 50th wedding anniversary. One of the hardest things about Bev's death was realizing I'd never celebrate 50 years of marriage. I said farewell to my marriage to Bev with a private 50th anniversary celebration and letter (found on Page 157 of the appendix). Then I could move on. After celebrating the 50th, as I drove back to San Jose, I called Caryl and told her I was ready to move on with the rest of my life. A year later we were engaged!*

That first retreat in January 2007 was to become a pattern. For the next two years I began the new year in this same place, and spent time praying, writing, and reading. I reviewed what I'd written the previous year, adding new journal entries and setting goals for the year before me.

As time went by and I began to heal, my priorities changed. These comments were part of my time with God in January 2009:

I don't think I will come back next year even though these retreats have been an important phase in my grief journey.

Will I continue the retreats? Yes but each year and location will be different based on my needs and circumstances.

Two years ago, the words of Psalm 4 were my plea: *"Answer me when I call to you, O my righteous God. Give me relief from my distress; be merciful to me and hear my prayer."*

Today, I resonate with Psalm 8: *"When I consider your heavens, the work of your fingers, the moon and stars, which you have set in place, what is man that you are mindful of him, the son of man that you care for him."*

My hope is that others can learn from my experience, which has taught me:

1. It is good to get away and be with God. The location could be your own home with no phone, no TV and no interruptions, or it could be a motel room, a retreat center, etc. The important thing is being alone with God.
2. Grieving is hard work. Leaning into your pain and embracing the grief is very hard work, but very healing.
3. Take time to put your thoughts on paper, even if you don't consider yourself a writer. Later, reading what was going on in your heart and mind and spirit will be healing.

4. Recognize that God's Word – the Scriptures – is the source of all wisdom, comfort and guidance for our lives. I could not have made it without Scripture.
5. Be honest with God and yourself. This is not a time to be pious! If you are angry, hurting, confused and at a loss for direction, tell God what you are feeling. He has heard it all! Say it loud and often and, if necessary, yell it - I did!
6. Make certain you plan for and find ways to leave your retreat with some takeaways, challenges and action items that will encourage your growth. For example, What did I learn? What will I concentrate on in the coming days and months? What still troubles me? Honesty doesn't stop when your time alone ends.

My dad, my companion in grief
   by Todd Goehner

My dad and I had been close before Mom died, but we got a lot closer afterward. Since her death, we talk nearly every day. Not only did the amount and frequency of our communication increase, but we began talking at a much deeper emotional level. Because honesty was central to our dialog, we could pick up the phone and connect whenever one of us was struggling. Which was often.

We had both lost the most important woman in our lives. Yes, our relationships with her were different, but I found myself experiencing so many things in similar ways as my dad. I found out new things about him (as I'm sure he did about me) and we established new bonds.

The simplest way to describe how my dad worked through my mom's death is this: He did it.

He dealt with it right from the get-go. I watched as he moved intentionally forward, not just moving forward to move forward but to move into healing. I was there the night after she died and he had already made some choices to help him move ahead. "OK" he said then, "I have a different life now. I've never been alone, but I need to adjust."

What concerned me the most about how Dad would handle things following Mom's death was that he had lost his home base. He counted on his wife to be his sounding board, the person he could talk to and work through things. Now that was gone. That loss was huge, especially emotionally. We kids took on that role somewhat, but it was nowhere near what he had shared with her for 50 years.

It was great to see family members and friends rally around my dad. Interestingly, some of the people I thought would be there for him weren't, but others I didn't expect surrounded him with care. And, it wasn't what they did or didn't say, but their presence in his life. The night after my mom's death my dad's place was filled with people, just being there for him.

The best decision I made after my mom died was telling myself I need to go to therapy. That made all the difference in my recovery. Prior to beginning with the therapist I was angry because no one could give me a concrete answer as to why Mom died. The therapist helped me focus on my loss and making it personal and real, every day. To the point of even saying out loud to myself, "Mom's dead, she's not coming back." I didn't want to be in denial about what had happened. At this point, more than three years later, it still hurts and it's still real, but I've moved forward.

Death teaches you the true meaning of "irreversible." You can't fix it (and we love to fix ourselves and others!) and you can't ignore it. We all understand death intellectually, but my mom's sudden and unexpected death hurt so deeply. Like my dad, my scenario for my parents didn't include him outliving her. I was completely unprepared.

There truly is life after death, even the death of a wife and a mother. It's easy – but unhealthy – to withdraw and not include others in your process. The natural inclination is to feel socially unacceptable and stay away from people. Those who truly love and care about you can be there with you, inside your circle of grieving.

Eighteen months that changed my life

As I look back on my grieving experience, I can clearly see the hand of God (although at first it did not appear to be anything other than pain.) In an 18-month period, I experienced more changes and challenges than I had faced during any year-and-a-half of my entire life.

The first, and hardest, change was Bev's death. I had never expected to outlive her. Like most husbands, I expected to precede my wife in death and, so, was totally unprepared for her death. Based on the Alzheimer's diagnosis by the Stanford University medical staff, I realized we were facing difficult times but did not anticipate I would be alone so quickly.

I had actually given a good deal of thought to the privilege I would have of caring for Bev, especially as I considered the many ways she had cared for me. I had read about the president of a Christian college who, upon his wife's diagnosis of Alzheimer's, had resigned and spent the next several years caring for her until her death. I wasn't sure I was up to the challenge but I was determined to try.

Health concerns

Six weeks after her death, on my birthday (December 22, a birth date I shared with Bev…we were the exact same age), I received a call from my doctor's office while driving with Terri. The nurse inquired as to whether I had an appointment scheduled with the doctor. I replied, "Yes, on the 26th." Her terse reply was: "That's good because you are diabetic." So much for bedside manner!

I was so surprised I almost ran off the road but managed to thank her. I did not share the news with Terri or any family member until after the appointment and the conclusion of the holidays.

I was scared. The health history of my extended family includes diabetes. My grandmother was diabetic, as were two of her sons – my uncles. I believe it contributed to the death of one of them. Two of my cousins had juvenile diabetes and one died at a relatively early age. So, I knew about the disease and its toll. Plus, I dreaded the possibility of insulin injections.

Before my appointment I prayed a lot and thought, "I can't give myself shots." To my surprise, my doctor declared me pre-diabetic and felt I could control my condition with diet and exercise. He challenged me to beat diabetes, which was just the challenge my competitive nature needed. Three years later – through diet and exercise – I am outside the diabetic range. But on December 22, 2006, I was scared.

My mother's final days

When Bev died my mother, Esther, lost both her daughter-in-law and her primary caregiver. (In fact, my mom was the last person Bev saw before she suffered a seizure in the parking lot of a fast-food restaurant.) She had faithfully taken care of my mother for seven years after we moved her to the San Jose area in 1999. After my father died in October 1998, it became apparent that Mom needed to be closer to a family member. The most logical move for her was to come north and be near us.

For all those years, Bev visited her while she was at the senior-living apartment. As her health began to fail, we hired an aide to help her two days a week. In 2004, it was necessary to move her into a nursing facility. Bev's duties increased as she did my mom's laundry and met regularly with the medical staff about her situation. Mom was difficult to deal with at times, but Bev continued to care for and love her unconditionally.

When Bev died, I did not tell my mother. She was in the beginning stages of dementia (and had become very confused in the summer of 2006 when I shared that one of her younger brothers had died). When she asked, "Where is Bev?" I would reply, "She's home." It was the truth but her "home" was probably not what my mom perceived.

In late 2006, Terri and I began taking on greater caregiver roles, trying to share the responsibilities. It became apparent to me we would have a difficult time maintaining this regimen. God intervened and on February 25, 2007, my mom died of old age.

I had the privilege of spending her last morning on earth with her. I sang her favorite hymns and read her the Scriptures she had underlined in her Bible. The nursing home was just across the street from our church, so two of our pastors were able to stop in and pray with her. Just a few hours later, she experienced what he prayed. (Please see "My Mom's Graduation" on Page 178 in the appendix for more about this remarkable woman's last hours with us.)

My mother's death left me with mixed emotions. I grieved her death, yet I was relieved that my care-giving responsibilities were completed. I was also saddened because I knew caring for my mom wore Bev down. She had spoken of the day when Mom would be with Jesus and we could concentrate on our life and marriage. I grieved because Bev never experienced that moment. I am almost certain when Mom got to heaven she asked Bev, "What are you doing here?"

A daughter's crisis

Twelve months later, in late February, my daughter, Terri, called me to say she had an important doctor's appointment the next day. She had found a large lump on her breast and her doctor had referred her to an oncologist to be tested for cancer.

I was stunned! "Oh, God, not another family member with a critical medical situation!"

During the next few hours, I frantically called family members and friends asking tor prayer. I gathered an e-mail prayer team, just as I had done for Bev. A few days later, I accompanied Terri to the appointment with the oncologist and heard the dreaded words, "You have breast cancer in your right breast and in your lymph nodes… probably late Stage 3."

Terri tried to keep a positive attitude, but had tears in her eyes. And so began another journey of critical health issues with a loved one. Terri was given chemo treatments, had a mastectomy, radiation and received special medication that forced her into menopause.

Through it all, she was incredibly brave and hardly missed any work.

I tried to be there for her but I knew she missed her mother; there was no way I could bridge that gap. God was extremely gracious and a group of women, some of whom belonged to her small group from church, rallied around her during her cancer fight. She rarely, if ever, went to a treatment alone.

On December 16, 2008, she received a call telling us she was cancer-free. What a celebration! To this day, she continues to be free of this terrible disease. (Please see my e-mail to our prayer team about Terri's situation on Page 202 in the appendix.)

—⁂—

Terri Goehner, Don and Bev's daughter

> *It is hard to watch your parent grieve because there isn't much you feel like you can do to help them. Fortunately, Dad wasn't afraid to show his pain and his loss. He was very open about what he was feeling and what he was dealing with. He didn't hide away and grieve alone, but continued to live (attend church, work, etc) while dealing with his loss.*
>
> *My concerns about Dad after Mom died were more on the practical side. What would he eat? Would he be able to do his own laundry and take care of the house? I wasn't sure he even knew how to grocery-shop or how to plan meals!*
>
> *I knew Dad had his work during the day, but worried about how he would spend his evenings. Would he be alone most of the time?*

I struggled, too. When Dad traveled, Mom and I used to spend Saturdays together shopping, having lunch, or just hanging out. It was hard to think about all those Saturdays without Mom. Shortly after Mom died and I was out shopping, I heard a young man call out, "Mom!" and it hit me: I would never use that word again to address someone.

When you lose a dad or a mom you become very protective of the remaining parent. I realized that if Dad died, I wouldn't have any parents left. That realization, along with other factors, helped Dad and I become closer, and spend more time together.

What helped Dad the most was people just being there. They didn't have to say anything (and were often quite honest, admitting that they didn't know what to say), but they allowed Dad to verbalize his grief, to cry, to talk, or just be silent. The guys who took him to lunch and coffee, or just called to check on him – those times were very important. Other widows and widowers, who came alongside Dad and helped him process and understand what he was facing, were also very helpful.

Our family faces still more challenges

Just one month after Terri's initial diagnosis, I received a call from my son, Todd. He no longer had a job and it was clear his termination was a poorly handled. (He had been an applicant for the position of executive director position of the social-service agency where he worked. Another person was chosen and two weeks after she arrived, Todd was released. He was devastated.) He had worked so hard to institute new programs that helped the unemployed return to the work force. I found myself, once again, being a caregiver.

My son has suffered many difficulties in his life and this just seemed so unfair. I prayed hard because Todd had deeply grieved the loss of his mother and I didn't know how he would respond to this new and huge disappointment. (Todd has since moved to a new agency and is flourishing in his new role.) Adding to my concern was the fact that he had just ended his engagement three months prior to his dismissal.

Finally, just four months later, Bev's sister, Jene, was also diagnosed with breast cancer. This occurred one month after she and her husband, Wes, had celebrated their 50th wedding anniversary. While I was somewhat removed from this situation, it was just another blow in the 18 months following Bev's death.

As these issues began to pile up I found myself realizing as I had sought to lean into the pain of grief, I was not totally aware of what that meant. Through it all, God was faithful. Even in the darkest moments (and there were many), I put my hope in God. He proved faithful.

Planning events that strengthened my new sense of normal

As I began my journey as a widower, I realized very rapidly I needed to be proactive. I had watched others retreat from people and events, and spend a good deal of time – too much, I thought – alone and apart from people. I was determined to find a balance between my time alone and interacting with people. I am, by nature, an extrovert and love being with people. But I also value my time alone, which is a surprise to many people who know me.

I set out to find ways to build new memories and discover life after the death of my spouse. One of the first was putting up the outdoor lights at Christmas. I had always done this, but never without Bev watching, helping me make certain the lights were all turned in a certain direction. As I told a grief-recovery class, it was the first time I could recall putting them up without some type of argument!

Because I was determined to recover, I scheduled my first personal retreat for January 2007. As discussed earlier, it was an important step in my ultimate recovery and healing.

As Valentine's Day approached I was concerned about spending that particular night alone. Bev and I had always made this a special date, with dinner, flowers, gifts, and time alone.

I decided I would plan a new event: an Un-Valentines party! I invited singles, another widower and divorced persons for an evening of food and fellowship at my house. We had a great time and I felt like I had passed over another hurdle in my recovery.

As I began learning to cook and entertain I asked a friend of my daughter's if she would be willing to be the guinea pig for my cooking education/adventure. I promised I would not poison her, but I didn't know how good the food would be. She agreed and a few weeks later, I invited her and my daughter, Terri, to dinner.

When they walked in, they found a table set with new placemats, linen napkins, flowers and chilled salad plates. I had enlisted the help of a longtime friend to put together a menu and I believe all were duly impressed.

That began a series of dinner parties over the next several months as I learned to prepare meals and entertain people. I have a small townhouse and my dining-room table seats four, the perfect size for excellent conversation. I received recipes from my friend Caryl and Tom's wife, Vivian. I was often on the phone during my preparations, asking for help and advice. I remember one evening when I could not reach either one and I had to figure it out on my own. Guess what? It worked out just fine and I had taken another step forward.

Special times for grandpa and grandsons

Shortly after Bev died, I decided I wanted to have a lasting memory and experience with each of my grandsons. A friend, who had recently been widowed, told me that she and a friend had taken one of their grandchildren to Washington, D.C. for a week, and it had been a great experience.

So, being ambitious and a big-thinker, I decided to take each of my grandsons to the East Coast for a history-themed trip when they turned 15. (Bev and I had done this in 1979 with our two youngest children, and it had been a great excursion.) It turned out that our trip took place just prior to the year in high school they would study U.S. history, making the trip a perfect introduction to their coursework.

In late June 2007, just after school ended, Keaton (my oldest grandson) and I flew to Boston to begin our adventure. For 10 days we toured the East, visiting special places in Boston and Springfield, Massachusetts (home of the Basketball Hall of Fame); New York; Philadelphia and Yorktown, Pennsylvania; Gettysburg and Williamsburg, Virginia; and last, but not least, Washington, D.C. Because Keaton is a gifted artist, we visited the Philadelphia Museum of Art. Afterward, he sketched what he had seen as we drove to our next destination.

Through an acquaintance from my alma mater, Westmont College, we received a behind-the-scenes tour of Congress and the Capitol. We capped it all off by watching the Fourth-of-July fireworks on the Washington Mall!

It was a very special bonding experience that continues to bless our relationship to this day. We had great conversations and I learned so much about this young man. On our last night together we prayed and had a very honest conversation about my future. I will always cherish this memory.

—⚭—

Keaton Hudson, Don and Bev's grandson

I was, and still am, very impressed by the way my grandfather handled everything that year and in the years that followed. My grandpa is my biggest role model in life and the individual whom I most admire. I had no fears or concerns about how my grandpa would handle the situation. I was confident that in the years that followed he would make the wisest decisions and do what was best for the family.

He didn't sulk around and wallow in his sorrow but made it clear he wasn't going to let his grief overpower him. He rejoiced in the fact that my grandma was in a better place and that we would all see her once again in heaven.

He didn't shut anyone out or shove himself into a corner and refuse help. One more thing I appreciated about the way Grandpa handled Nama's death was he let others know he needed help in dealing with her death. He made himself vulnerable. To me, that takes serious character.

What hit me the hardest after she died was realizing Nama was no longer a part of my life. Being Don and Bev's first grandson gave me two extra years to bond with my grandparents before my brothers came along. My grandmother and I shared a pretty special relationship, and when she passed away I no longer had this special woman who cared about me so much and passed on so much unconditional love to us grandkids. I'm learning to rejoice in my memories of her and now, three years later, I can even laugh about all the funny stories we shared.

I'm glad Grandpa had family and friends to help. The more people my grandfather was surrounded with, who loved him and cared for him, the better. My grandfather has made an impact on a huge amount of people, and many of them made themselves available to him when they heard about the death of his wife.

In the summer of 2009, I made a similar trip with my second grandson, Taylor. The boys are different, of course, so I tried to make this trip fit Taylor's personality and interests. He and I also went to the Basketball Hall of Fame, but we spent almost as much time at a store in Springfield, Mass., where he learned about making writing instruments. (As a freshman wood-shop student, Taylor had discovered his gift in this area.) We also went to an amusement park where he could engage in one of his loves: riding roller coasters.

During this stop, he got to meet some second cousins, one of which rode all the coasters with him. I watched!

Taylor loves big cities so we spent more time in New York City and we got tickets to an off-Broadway production (making all his friends envious and me an instant hero). We also saw historic sites in Philadelphia and Washington. This was another great bonding time, with many wonderful conversations as well. Since then, Taylor has begun making pens (with the efficiency and capacity of an assembly line!) and has them displayed at a stationery story in his hometown of Santa Barbara.

Living the new normal

Perhaps the most difficult event in my new normal was celebrating my 50th wedding anniversary, alone! June 28, 2008, marked the 50th anniversary of our marriage. Bev and I had looked forward to this date for years, and had planned to take our entire family to central Oregon for a week's vacation to commemorate the occasion. Obviously, her death changed those plans.

As the date approached, I sought to find an appropriate way to mark this life milestone, while continuing to lean into the pain of my own grief.

I drove to one of our favorite towns, Cambria, on the central Calif. coast. I stayed at our favorite hotel on the beach and ate at our favorite restaurant. We had a family joke that whenever we ate out, we would always end up at a table next to someone with a loud voice. I had that same experience and smiled as I recalled how Bev would have leaned over and said, "He never learned to use his 'inside' voice." Somehow, I think she was smiling in heaven.

It was during that weekend I wrote a 50th-anniversary letter to Bev (found on Page 157 in the appendix) as well as letters to my three children. I wrote, with tears streaming down my cheeks, thanking God for our 48 years of marriage and two years of relationship prior to that. I realized God had given us 50 years after all!

As part of the anniversary celebration, I had a friend create a personal memory album for each of my children. It contained pictures of them with their mother, some of the cards we received after her death and a personal letter from me. (These letters can be read in the appendix, beginning on Page 162.) I wanted them to understand how significant this weekend and anniversary was to me.

LESSONS LEARNED

I found other healthy ways to bring balance to my relationships. With my kids, there was a fine – and sometimes shifting – line between being the dad they needed and the Don I needed. For example, more than once I felt like I had to provide things for them that, in the past, our family couldn't afford. I'm generous by nature and sometimes probably gave too much. A person's strengths, of course, can easily become their weaknesses, but I'm getting more balanced in this area.

I haven't always been good at knowing when to step back and let my kids and others go through their own process without my involvement. Caryl has helped me learn the value and ways of doing this.

Several women from our church came alongside Terri and ministered to her in ways I could not. They listened to her pain and took an active interest in her recovery. Todd sought out intensive counseling for nearly a year and it was a huge help for him. Although his church wasn't as helpful or understanding as it might have been, Todd and I grieved together. Trina was blessed by the love of several women from her church. Among other things, they drove the 10-hour round trip to be a support for Trina during Bev's service.

Celebrating Bev's life

On the first anniversary of her death I wanted to celebrate Bev's life with my family. I invited the family to join me in Santa Barbara and asked them all to meet at Trina's home.

Prior to the date, a friend helped me select gifts for each member of the family. I bought engraved necklaces for my daughters and gave each one a diamond from their mother's ring. My son and son-in-law received engraved clocks and the three grandsons received a photo album filled with pictures of them alone with their grandmother. Each album was engraved, "I love you, Nama." (As a toddler, Keaton had been unable to pronounce "Grandma," so "Nama" became her beloved name.) I was wearing my wedding band with Bev's diamond on my right hand as part of our celebration.

The evening was fabulous! I rented a stretch limo and when the driver and I showed up, my youngest grandson, Carter, came running out and said, "Is that for us?" He climbed in and soon became enamored with all the things he found – music, padded seats, soft drinks, etc.

We drove to a local restaurant for dinner and on the way, Todd exclaimed, "We have done this before. Dad, you rented a similar limo to celebrate your 25th anniversary. And, I bet we are going to the Harbor Restaurant." I replied, "Todd, this was such a special time, I wanted to repeat what we did 25 years ago."

We had a great dinner and then headed to my suite in a nearby hotel where they opened their gifts and we spent time remembering all the funny things Bev had done. It was a time to laugh and we rocked the room with some funny stories (Bev could be very funny... without even trying.) It is a memory I will never forget and I hope is a memory for my children and grandsons as well.

In an effort to honor Bev and make an impact in the lives of young adults, I endowed two college scholarships in her honor. Our family finds it ironic (and joyful) that Bev, who was not a college graduate, is honored by these scholarships. I have discovered these celebrations and scholarships have helped keep her memory alive.

The Bev Goehner Endowed Scholarship at Westmont College is given annually to a student going into elementary education and who, in the minds of the faculty, is the most promising future teacher of children. Bev loved children and this seemed fitting. The second recipient has just been named and Bev's legacy lives on. At Simpson University, the Bev Knowles Goehner Scholarship is given to a student in the preschool education program.

Inviting people to share in my grief

It may be apparent to you I have been somewhat unorthodox in my approach to grieving. It is said "widows grieve and widowers rebound;" I was determined not to fit that widower stereotype.

Since I had built an e-mail prayer list during Bev's illness, I continued it after her death and, at the suggestion of a friend, continued to update people for a year. (Some of those e-mails are contained in the appendix, beginning on Page 134.) It allowed people to know how I was doing and helped them talk about Bev. It went a long way toward providing an answer to the often-asked question, "How are you doing, Don?"

I attended a grief-recovery class at my church along with my daughter, Terri. Two years later I had the opportunity to address the class and share my experience. (Please see my notes from the presentation, beginning on Page 184 in the appendix.)

Several people had given me permission to call them on their cell phones – anytime - and I did so on a few occasions, in order to have a live person with whom to interact. These men became an informal accountability group to whom I reported and with whom I discussed my feelings quite openly.

One of these was my son-in-law, Steen Hudson. Steen was an anchor during my first year of being alone. He seemed to know just when to call and would simply say, "Just checking in." He was a godsend and I am extremely grateful. Others included Ed McDowell, Gary Low, Tom Nelson and Gayle Beebe. These and others gave me the wonderful gift of allowing me to grieve -- without being pathetic.

LESSONS LEARNED

It's interesting that the people who got it – meaning, they really cared about and understood what I was going through - were from all walks of life and many different situations. Many of those who were there for me had lost a spouse or someone very close to them. I discovered that the more pain they had lived with, the more they understood me and my pain. There were some who I expected would get it and would come alongside, but they didn't. Honestly, that hurt.

Some folks went beyond sensitivity and began walking with me. Like Ed McDowell, one of The Goehner Group's associates and Warm Beach Camp's executive director. He is the godliest man I know, but he made his wisdom, insight, and love available. He was there for my journey and still is today.

About four months after Bev's death, in the course of my work, I interviewed a woman who is a trustee of Mount Hermon, a Christian conference center in California's Santa Cruz Mountains. Sue Cairns had lost her husband, Bruce, to cancer just three months before Bev's death. In fact, I attended the memorial service for Bruce.

Up to then we had been acquaintances, but on that particular afternoon we began to share our experiences and losses with one another. We soon began to meet on a regular basis and agreed to become prayer partners. That relationship exists to this day. Sue is a godly woman who had turned her tragedy into a ministry to young women and to widows in India. I greatly admire her and will always be grateful for her influence in my life. In fact, she is the person who helped me plan the first anniversary event in remembrance of Bev.

I soon realized part of my recovery needed to include writing. I was under no illusions that recording my experiences would become a book. I just wanted to journal my journey for reading later and to leave my perspective on Bev's legacy for the family. As I poured myself into the work, however, I became aware this story might become helpful to others. That's when I began to believe it could become a book.

Coming to faith, growing in God

As a young boy and teenager, I attended church every Sunday because that is what our family did. I even went on Wednesday nights to prayer meeting. I remember having an interest in God but I never experienced a personal relationship with God.

In high school, I began to live a double life. I had all the right words at church, but I was quite different at school and, among other things, got quite good at telling dirty jokes. Because my father told me I couldn't play sports if he ever caught me drinking, I avoided alcohol. Nevertheless, I was anything but a Christian.

Following my conversion, just after my 17th birthday, a new Don appeared. God got hold of my life and the first positive step was being discipled by a teacher who later introduced me to Bev. Within a few months I was attending a Youth for Christ training school in Kansas City. By the fall of my freshman year in college I was directing Youth for Christ Bible Clubs in Yakima, Wash.

After graduating from Westmont in 1960, two events shaped the rest of my life. I became a full-time staff member with Youth for Christ and my daughter, Terri, was born. To this day, I have a heart for ministry and a desire to be a dad and enjoy family.

My walk with God

Bev's death put my faith to the test. Was God sufficient? I had been taught he was and at times had sensed it. But, quite frankly, I often was doing God's work in my own strength, trying to be a husband, dad and Christian leader by my own efforts.

Her death shook me to the core. I remember walking, crying and praying God would help me. I felt guilty about all the time I had been away from my wife and children because of business and ministry travel obligations. I questioned whether I had been a good husband and father.

One day, on my first retreat, I stopped and looked at the ceiling and simply said, "God I can't do this on my own." With my palms facing up I cried out, "I will rely on you alone." That began a new journey with the Father, the Son and the Holy Spirit.

I have a new reliance on God's Word. I have developed a new discipline of Scripture reading and prayer. I have just completed a year in which I began every day in God's Word. That was truly a first for me! I don't say this proudly but, rather, with a grateful heart. Without God's Word, I would not be where I am today. It is alive and real and I am committed to following it, even when its instructions to me are hard.

I have learned a new meaning for the word "forgiveness." Some time back, I was going through a difficult time because some contemporaries of mine were accusing me of actions that were simply not true. One Sunday morning, our pastors did an illustrated sermon about the woman caught in adultery, as described in John 8. At the end of the service, the senior pastor challenged us: "If there are people in your life who need your forgiveness, pick up the rock at the end of the pew and bring it to the altar." I did just that and as I dropped the rock on the altar, I sensed a great release. Since then I have experienced the power of God's forgiveness – granting it to people as well as receiving it from others.

Prayer has become more alive and I realize it is simply a conversation with God. He can handle my anger, fears and attitudes. I have had all of those and been very frank in my conversational prayer. God has met me, even though at times I have felt like the psalmist who cried to a God who seemed silent.

I discovered most of the Psalms conclude with the writer reaffirming his trust in God. That is what I have experienced, too. I still have many unanswered prayers, but I have learned through experience that God is both sovereign and faithful. Often his greatest and most satisfying answer to my prayer is simply his strengthening presence.

One of the major changes I have experienced is my participation in communion. I confess that prior to Bev's death, taking part in the Lord's Supper was little more than going through the motions. As I began to observe my first communion following her death, I began to weep as I realized the incredible sacrifice Christ made for my sins. Even more importantly, I realized that without his crucifixion, there would have been no resurrection. Without the resurrection, I would never see Bev again. By the end of that communion service, I was rejoicing!

Kevin, the pastor who spent the first 36 hours following Bev's death at my side, said something profound I have never forgotten. "Don, rather than trying to live one day at a time, as everyone will tell you, live a half day at a time." I began doing that and it was my lifeline for weeks.

Today, as I am writing this, I realize again that all I have is today. So, I continue to try to live in the moment – even when it is painful. I must constantly remind myself that God expects my faithfulness in each situation as I experience it. That's my goal, even though I don't always reach it.

New beginnings

January 3, 2009

It's Saturday morning and I am wrapping up my time at the cottage on Whidbey Island. This marks my third personal retreat since my wife's death. I come here to reflect and find out what I can learn from this special experience.

Two years ago I was less than two months removed from Bev's death and literally holding on by my fingertips. I had just met with my doctor and been told that I was diabetic.

On December 31, I had a very emotional experience when I lost Bev's house keys. The keys were one of my last personal, everyday connections to her. That same evening, I was informed that my flight was cancelled and I would not leave until New Years Day afternoon.

When I arrived on the morning of January 2, 2007, after spending the night with Wes and Jene, I was agitated, frustrated, scared, and lonely. For the next few days, I prayed, read, cried and wrote. I spent the first 24 hours in silence and I will always treasure that time because it set the stage for God to touch my heart in very significant ways. I have reread my journal from that experience and found it was a turning point in my grief journey.

Now, two years later, I have a very different mind and spirit as God continues to heal me. So much has happened and I give the praise and glory to God.

This time I wanted to accomplish a few key things:

1. Finish my journal of Bev's last year, *"10 Months and 10 Days"*
2. Work on The Goehner Group's Management Service Plan
3. Work on the company's mission statement
4. Review progress on the personal goals I set for myself in 2007 and 2008, and set my goals for 2009
5. Update the plan for my memorial service
6. Spend time reading and reflecting
7. Spend time in God's Word and prayer
8. Begin journaling on a regular basis again

Nearly all of these, particularly the first five, have been accomplished. I have also spent some time reading and reflecting, but that is ongoing. I have made a commitment to read five Psalms and one Proverb each day for the next three months (thanks to Mark Platt's suggestion). That process has begun and I will recheck in late March.

I am determined to check my goals quarterly, rather than waiting until the end of each year. I will begin journaling again, but I plan to use my computer. For a variety of reasons I think it is more practical for me. I will also write on paper, but I hope the two methods combined will give me the soul time I need.

A number of other practical things are different this time. Two years ago, I cooked packaged meals because I was clueless in the kitchen. This time, I prepared healthy meals from scratch and had fun doing it.

In 2007, after 24 hours of silence, I spent a great deal of time speaking on the phone with people who could identify with my grief. Janet Anderson and Joan Newlon were particularly helpful. Last year I spoke with several people and, in particular, spent time on the phone with Sue Cairns (who is on a journey similar to mine). I also got acquainted with Sarah Kravet, who was leaving the Admirals Club at that time. In addition, Caryl Taylor and I spoke a lot as we explored our relationship. In both 2007 and 2008, Ed McDowell and I had meaningful conversations.

Sue Cairns, Don's friend

My husband died three months before Bev's death. Because we both had lost a spouse, our friendship helped us grow, despite our circumstances. Don and I prayed faithfully for one another, which was a huge help.

Don trusted the Lord, had hope for the future and refused to dwell in a personal pity party. He was thinking about his future and planning on how to accomplish some things in his life, a life that no longer included Bev.

All in all, I felt he handled the transition from married to widowed well. Although I felt he was sometimes rushing the grieving process, he seemed to know what he needed to do.

Don and I both attended grieving classes after our spouses died, giving us more resources and perspective as we moved forward in the process. Don stayed close to several longtime friends and his family members. He often called and visited his children and grandchildren, and spent time with Bev's family members, too - I think he liked being with the people who knew and loved her.

At this year's retreat I have only placed four calls since arriving at the cabin. I called Del and Darren because I could not find the key. (As is typical of me, I didn't look close enough.) I made no calls on New Years Day as I watched football, wrote and read. Last night I called Wes to confirm that I will visit them today, spoke with Caryl and got caught up.

There were some other noticeable changes. I spent New Year's Eve on the Island at the Saratoga Inn and ate dinner alone at the Edgeclif, just across the road. I spoke with Caryl and we prayed together regarding 2009. That was a sweet time.

By now, I have developed some routines. I followed my walking route on Thursday and Friday. Although it was wet one day and quite brisk the next, both excursions were very invigorating and enjoyable.

LESSONS LEARNED

I'm thankful, for not only how God has carried me on this journey, but also for how he made me. I've learned that the more I grow, the challenges I face will increase. And, I wouldn't have it any other way. I don't think I've reached my capacity for what I can be as a person, following God.

Proverbs 24:10 reminds us, "If you falter in times of trouble, how small is your strength!" Through times sad and glad, my strength is the Lord. He is my only refuge. I've said, "God, as I look back on these three years, I'm grateful for where I am now and the pain I've experienced."

I came here quite needy in 2007, and was headed for another memorial service in Wenatchee when I left the island. Today, I feel healthy and tuned up for 2009. I am still needy, of course, but in different ways. The prayer list from my time here reflects those issues of need and growth.

The biggest difference is that I can't stop saying thank you to the Father for his goodness to me. I am so blessed. I do not know how many more years -- or even days -- I have, but I can only offer praise to my God who delivers me.

I don't know if I will come back next year because this phase in my life may have passed by then. Only time will tell. I will, however, schedule another retreat this year in a different location. These times with God and alone are important for my mind, body and soul.

I go home to face a new year, assured God loves me, cares for me and answers prayer. I face a great deal of difficulty but he is sufficient!!

Some final thoughts

Now, on January 2, 2009, as I sit here on Whidbey Island reading what I've written over the last 18 months, a great deal of it seems unreal. Some of details have blurred, but the central theme is strong. God called Bev home sooner than any of us wanted. I, along with all her family and friends, miss her dearly. Her grandsons and our family tell funny stories about her antics and her sense of humor. Christmas will never be the same. Our church has lost its hospitality queen.

Good things, however, have happened as a result of Bev's death. Todd is the not the man he was before; his mom's death basically shocked him into moving forward with his life. I now take care of the house and even remember family birthdays. I honored Bev by establishing two college scholarships in her memory. Terri has fought cancer and appears to be winning. Trina looks and acts more like Bev every day, giving me an unexpectedly unique way to remember Bev. Steen is moving closer to joining our company full time and allowing me to move on from that chapter of my life. My grandsons are becoming wonderful young men.

Thanks for reading. This is a story of God's faithfulness to a young couple from central Washington who met as teenagers, fell in love and spent nearly 50 years together. Through it all, God's Word has been our guide and the authority for our lives. When Bev became ill, we claimed a passage from Isaiah which has comforted and sustained me in my grief journey:

"When you pass through the waters, I will be with you; and when you pass through the rivers, they will not sweep over you. When you walk through the fire, you will not be burned; the flames will not set you ablaze. For I am the Lord, your God, the Holy One of Israel, your Savior…Do not be afraid for I am with you." Isaiah 43:2-3; 5a

Where – and who – am I now?

After more than three years since losing my life partner, it's fair to ask, "Where are you on your journey now?" You'll find part of the answer to that question in the letter I wrote to Bev, "It's been three years," on Page 165 in the appendix.

In many ways, I am the same person – passionate about God and life, competitive, desiring to be a good father and grandfather. And, I still get frustrated when mechanical things like computers don't work.

In other ways, however, I am completely different. I don't think anyone can experience what I have gone through without being changed – either for good or for bad.

I am still living day by day…trying to live with my palms up, learning to trust God. This past year has been a difficult one in business and I have had to make some painful decisions. I am walkng by faith and the future is cloudy. Yet, I look forward, trusting God for what he has in store for me.

I am aware of one thing: my life will change yet again in just a few months. I am now engaged to be married to Caryl Taylor, a friend of 30 years. Yes, the Caryl who helped me learn to cook and who has allowed me to grieve. We have expanded our friendship to love and, finally, to our commitment to spend the rest of our lives together. Caryl has never been married (satisfying one of my criteria for remarriage) and I believe God saved her for me. Even this has been hard, because one member of my family is opposed to our marriage.

Finally, despite all that has happened, I want to speak clearly and strongly about the reality of my experience these past three years. I have been greatly blessed by God. My wife was an incredible gift, as are my children, grandsons, and my son-in-law. Through all that has happened – difficult as well as joyous – I am determined to live an attitude of gratitude as I move forward, one half-day at a time.

APPENDIX

My letter to Bev
Read at her memorial service, November 18, 2006

Dear Sweetie,

We are just about to start the service. The church is full and we just finished watching the slideshow of your life. We are here to honor you, celebrate your life of service, give praise and glory to God, and experience the hope of the resurrection.

It has been eight days since your "graduation," so I guess that translates to about 8000 biblical years. The book of Hebrews talks about a great cloud of witnesses and today we are part of that reality. Many friends are here: extended family, Goehner Group team members, past YFC staff, clients, Westmont trustees, Young Life board members, church friends, and people from our neighborhood.

But down front and center are the people who really counted in your life: Terri, Todd and Trina, "The Three TLs," as I like to call them. Steen, your beloved son-in-law is here, as well as Char, Todd's special girlfriend and, most importantly, your grandsons.

We are all scrubbed and proud. I got a haircut; Todd bought his first suit; Keaton is wearing the suit that he wore to his first prom; Taylor and Carter are wearing ties; and yes, Taylor has on long pants for the occasion.

Someone has described you as someone who was born to be a mother, but especially to be a grandmother. Keaton was your first grandchild and you put together scrapbooks of his early years. A bookmark he made at age 3 remains in your Bible to this day. You giggled at his baldness, big vocabulary and phrases like "Can you bereeve it?"

You were so proud when he graduated from junior high and laughed when you heard he was talking on the phone to girls. There was one in particular, but, of course, the conversations were all about "homework!" That reminded you of Trina, who always called her new boyfriends "just friends." I'm sorry you didn't get to see Keaton run cross-country because he is good. He is also the one who named you "Nama" and he is very proud of that.

Taylor is here, without any casts or snakes. You had a special place in your heart for him who, like you, is a middle child. I remember returning from a business trip (during which Taylor stayed with you) and finding I'd become a bit of an outsider looking in; you and he had developed a new and special bond. You were thrilled when he led the pledge of allegiance at his sixth-grade promotion and were especially proud when Trina reported that Taylor had gotten straight A's. (You knew how hard he had worked to earn those marks.)

That brings me to Carter. I will never forget your last visit to Santa Barbara. We had just received your final diagnosis and it had been a day and night of tears as we drove south. Everything cleared up Saturday morning when you saw Carter and he sat in your lap watching Taylor's soccer game. I have always said that he is you in a male body. He looks like you and has the same confidence you had as a child. He was never afraid to try new words and some of them were so unique, like "highway control" instead of "highway patrol." You and Terri even made a list of them, so we would not forget. He loved to hear you talk about his special words!

Your youngest grandson wasn't the only one who had fun with words. You had your own vocabulary of phrases, like:
- Fibber McGee's drawer
- Mind your P's and Q's

- Get the grump out of your toes and the peanut butter out of your ears
- Forty-leven (a really big number)
- Go brush your snags
- Ready to go Mimi's?

Some of your signature words came with actions, too! The grandsons' favorite was "Goggles Pisano." While driving, you put your face over the steering wheel and pretended to drive erratically, causing the boys to giggle. They loved it!

Your confidence was one of the first things that attracted me to you. You would try anything. When your sister, Jene, successfully begged your parents to take her someplace, they would find you in the backseat of the car, dressed, and quietly waiting to go, too!

I have been asked, "What was the first thing you noticed about Bev?" My answer never changes: your eyes. Brown and full of sparkle. I always knew how you felt about things by looking into your eyes.

Like the time early in our marriage when you sat me down and gently, but firmly, told me I was a jerk. That was one of the very first come-to-Jesus meetings you called me to. Those eyes could send – and reinforce – a message from a long way off. Once, during a ski lesson I insisted you take, those eyes burned into mine from a hundred feet away as you shouted, "This is stupid! Don't you ever do this to me again!!"

Your beautiful eyes, which I could sit and look into for hours at a time, began to fade in the last few months and were usually filled with tears.

Wow, the memories. Especially this year, as you slowly, then more rapidly, began to slip into confusion and increasing physical pain.

You were known by many names: "Slatz" (your e-mail password), "Bebbs," "Beaver Meadow" (the literal translation of your given name, Beverly), and Trina's favorite, "Sarge, the man in charge".

My favorite was "Sweetheart." During your last morning in the hospital I said, "Good morning, Sweetheart."

You replied, "What did you call me?"

"Sweetheart!" you replied, "You never called me that before."

I had to step into the hall while I wept.

I still remember our first date on March 3, 1956. I was so pleased to be with you and after that I never dated anyone else again. You told me, years later, that your mom said, "Bev, I know he's nice, but he is so homely." Yes, Sweetheart, you had hope for me when others didn't. You even loved me when I wore a yellow sport jacket with a pocket handkerchief bearing the words, "Business is good."

You should be aware that the people here today have seen the wedding picture, so now they know. Yes, that picture Todd would show our guests during our Christmas parties in Ventura, when you would point to me and say that I was your "first" husband. What a privilege for me to have been your husband for 48 years!

Your confidence and faith in me allowed you to love me unconditionally, even when I didn't deserve it. You were my biggest cheerleader, sacrificing to help my ministry succeed. You took in ironing, babysat children, sold tennis shoes over the phone (that didn't last very long!) and drove dumpy cars (one of my greatest thrills was when I was able to buy you your first new car), never complaining, always praying.

One Sunday, when we were down to our last can of soup, you asked me to give thanks and then rejoiced when someone came to the door while we were eating to bring a check that kept our ministry going. You wanted me to pursue my calling and you were at my side all the way.

Remember when the car engine caught on fire in the driveway? After carefully locking the kids in the car, you ran into the house to call the fire department!

Honey, we are recalling lots of stories today, most of which are very funny. Nearly everyone who has called me has a "Bev story," each one enhanced by your willingness to laugh at yourself. You can relax, though - I am not going to tell the "mouse story."

One of your greatest joys is that we shared the same birth date, December 22. You were excited to discover that Steen's birthday was one day earlier and that he was one day old in 1956, when we were engaged. Every birthday from now on will be different; bittersweet, as I am unable to celebrate with my life partner.

We spent a lot of time in the car together, and even ended up in traffic school with each other. Although I believe you forgave me, you never forgot the time I talked a highway patrolman into giving you a ticket. I explained to him that you had become arrogant and self-righteous as you compared your driving record to mine. The rest of that drive south of Salinas was pretty quiet.

One of the e-mails I received talked about how you are now "dancing in heaven." That is great, because that means you finally found a partner who can actually dance! You loved to remind me that the dance instructor said I was hopeless. One of my funniest memories involves you dancing joyfully in front of your dad (the same dad who had forbidden dancing during your youth) at your nephew's wedding.

I am certain you have joined the heavenly chorus and are a featured soloist. I am sorry that people who knew you later in life never heard you as singing those wonderful solos in our church of 2000 in southern Calif.

Honey, what a special year you had. In God's wisdom and providence we made a trip to the Southeast to work with Young Life and got to see special friends from the '70s, followed by visits to the Biltmore and the Billy Graham Center (The Cove) in Ashville, N.C. You got to spend a special week with the grandsons in Santa Barbara while Steen and Trina were on a cruise to Mexico. And finally, a special weekend at your favorite spot – Cambria.

While attending our 50-year high-school reunions you were surprised at how much others had aged. It's true - you looked younger and, in my opinion, were the most beautiful woman there.

That time was especially meaningful because of the wonderful three days we spent with your lifelong friend, Ardelle, and her husband, Lee. She whispered in my ear as we parted, "Take special care of my friend, she is slipping away." I think that a week ago on Friday, God decided he could care for you better than me.

Little did I know when I signed up for the Mount Hermon cruise that it would be our last vacation together. You loved it and we had a wonderful time cruising, eating, laughing, and being together. We met new friends and spent time with Bob and Carol Kraning, who we hadn't seen in a long, long time. I had the stewards sing "Happy Birthday" to you as a joke (your birthday was four months away), not knowing that that would be my last opportunity to celebrate your birthday. My joke turned out to be a fine tribute to you, one I won't forget.

It was on our trip that I became convinced that darker days were ahead. Terri had written out a list of your outfits so you'd know what to wear, and I arranged your clothes for each day and occasion.

What a privilege to serve you, rather than you serving me.

I have two cards you gave me recently and both reflect you perfectly. The first one reads, "Happy Father's Day. I couldn't find a better husband and you know what a great shopper I am."

You loved bargains. You hid jackets on the racks at Nordstrom until they reached the price you wanted. I remember you showing me a jacket for which you paid $15 and you proudly announced, "It started at $150!" Your children are certain that Big Lots and Target have reduced their staff since you no longer shop there. The returns department at each of the stores where you shopped will have nothing to do.

The second card says, "Think of this little card as a great big hug." You added, "I really miss you a lot. Can we have a play day soon?"

You loved it when I was home. Our walks, our talks and the recent conversation about our wedding vows, including the part about "in sickness and in health."

Just so you know, I am trying to follow the rules of the house: put the toilet seat down, turn off the heat, take out the trash, leave the outside light on at night and don't splash on the mirrors.

But since you have graduated we have broken one rule: there has been more than one person in the kitchen at a time. You lovingly called it a one-butt kitchen, and only yours was to be in there. Well, you know what? It takes several of us to do what you did by yourself!

Christmas is coming and, boy, did you love that time of year! Listening to music, enjoying a fire in the fireplace, baking your special applesauce cake, wrapping gifts and cooking. At Christmas your uniqueness shone through magnificently. You hid gifts and sometimes forgot to wrap them. Every year someone would open a gift and find that it belonged to someone else. Terri was upset one year because she liked what she opened but it was intended for Trina! I have found gifts you purchased for giving this year...ones you probably got right after Christmas last year! But our finest memory was your annual announcement: "This year it is going to be a smaller Christmas. And I really mean it!" And then there would be more than ever.

Honey, this year it *will* be a smaller Christmas, because the biggest part of our family's Christmas celebration – you – will be missing.

There is so much more to tell, but we need to start our worship of God and our celebration of you. Honey, you lived out our life verse, John 15:16. *"You did not choose me but I chose you and appointed you to go and bear fruit that would remain."*

Bev, you are a woman of integrity, you could not tell a lie. You were faithful - to God, to me, to our children, to our grandchildren and our friends. A friend told me that you were her inspiration for being a mother and others have said you were their model for being a grandmother.

You were also a beautiful woman. People who saw your picture often commented, "Don, she is **beautiful**." You were an incredible mother and grandmother.

We will all miss you. Terri has lost her best friend. Todd will miss his beautiful mother. Trina is so much like you and allowed you to be so involved in her boys' lives, but now that influence is gone. Steen loved you and adored having you iron his shirts (and even paying for his laundry when you couldn't do it anymore.) And Char, of course, who loves our family, but especially you.

I am thrilled that your enlarged heart is healed, even though it leaves a whole in my heart big enough to drive a truck through. I am thrilled that God has wiped away all your tears because in the last few months I saw more tears than in the first 48 years of our marriage. It killed me to hear a catch in your voice as we ended our long-distance calls when I was travelling that final week of your life.

Giving you to God the night before you died was the hardest thing I have ever done, but it was the right thing to do.

We always understood there were two ways to do things: the wrong way and Bev's way. You planned this service and we are going to do it your way. Dance and sing well, my love. I love you, I miss you and will never forget you.

Love,
Don

Anniversary letter to Bev

June 28, 2008

Dear Sweetheart,

I am writing from the Fog Catcher Inn in Cambria where we spent many happy times. Wonderful times alone, with Tom and Viv, with friends, and, once, with our entire family. I chose to come here because I wanted to be in one of our favorite places on the 50th anniversary of our wedding day.

I still remember that day. It was warm, almost hot. I played golf with Tex and Gene Sweeney and washed my car while you were busy getting the church ready. The night before at the rehearsal, it had seemed like a dream that in 24 hours we would be man and wife. As I look back on that day, I had no idea what I was getting into and you probably didn't either. We knew were in love and that we had committed ourselves to each other.

Today is a bittersweet day. You and I had often talked about celebrating our 50th with our family, and had never really discussed a large party. Little did I know that today and this weekend the event would be a party of one. Honey, I wanted to be alone and get away to reflect and think, as well as to celebrate in my own way.

So I chose the Fog Catcher and last night I ate at the Sow's Ear, the restaurant we always enjoyed. I did the "early" special meal, in memory of you. Sure enough, there was a gentleman at the next table talking loudly! I remember how someone with a loud voice in a restaurant would always irritate you. It seemed fitting that I would experience the same thing, alone.

So much has changed in the last 19 months. Somehow, I think

you know and if you don't, it probably isn't important because you are with God, the Father, the Son and the Holy Spirit.

Terri will have surgery on July 9 to remove one breast. She has been so brave as she has fought breast cancer. She has lost her hair but not her dignity. She is surrounded now by many women, surrogate mothers and sisters, but I know she has missed you throughout this battle. I have done the best I can but I am a dad and not her mom. I have had to face the possibility that I could lose her as I did you. My faith continues to be challenged.

Todd is unemployed after losing his job at LSS. The termination was handled very unprofessionally. He was a top candidate for the executive director position, but after the new person was selected she decided she didn't want Todd or his expertise (which she lacked). It has been a hard three months but he has responded well. His new condo is terrific and you would love it. As he says, "Mom would be proud, I keep my blinds open!" I have had to help him financially. He and I are quite close.

Trina is going through a tough time after working for Steen at Elings Park for several months. As you know, she is incredibly talented and some of the employees who felt threatened by her skills decided she was getting special privileges because she was Steen's wife. So, Steen felt he had to release her. It has been tough on everybody but I believe they will get through it.

Steen is pushing hard to join our company full time by January 1. He is working for The Goehner Group part time, and doing a great job. He is tired of working in a non-profit organization where he has to deal with a volunteer board, many of whom are not qualified to function in that capacity. I am not sure we can afford to bring him on, so Fred, Steen, and I have a lot of work to do. Steen and Ed were planning to join TGG in three years, but we are looking are a much different scenario these days.

Your grandsons are growing up – quickly and vertically! Taylor is nearly 5'9" and Keaton is about the same size - they would tower over you. Carter hasn't grown in stature but he is quite the young man.

Keaton is incredibly handsome and quite a contrast to his earlier (and bald!) years. He is a great artist and I've proudly hung one of his paintings in my office. His love for sports has diminished, but he surfs. And drives! He has Steen's old car and appears to be a responsible driver. He will play soccer at San Marcos this year. At one point, Keaton got involved with the wrong crowd and made some poor choices, but appears to be turning things around and doing fine. I am still praying that God will lead him in a path of ministry.

You'd be thrilled with Taylor's development as a young man. He is still not a consistent student, but is becoming a great athlete and is working out with the San Marcos High basketball team. He has played his last competitive soccer (as an all star, again!) but will be playing volleyball at San Marcos. He and Trina have a great relationship because of his sense of humor. He just graduated from La Colina (and was one of two students who did not pose for the graduation picture). He does not like to be the center of attention and is still a slug…but a lovable one.

That brings me to Carter. He is the most active of the three, playing soccer (an all star this year), water polo, and, now, golf. He made the Junior PGA team and plays tournaments at all the nice courses in Santa Barbara. He is very determined, so much so that he improved his score significantly enough in one month he made the team!

Adults love him and Glen Adams takes him golfing quite often. In fact, Carter recently played with Glen and two other older men. One of them called and left Steen a message about what an incredible young man Carter is. He is a junior lifeguard this summer (for the third time), so between that and golf he is one busy boy. He graduated from the sixth grade last week. He did not have a good experience his last two years and is looking forward to La Colina because a lot of church friends will be there.

Then there's me.

Babe, I think you would be proud of me. I have learned to cope and live alone. It has not been easy, but everyone seems amazed at what I've learned to do. I love cooking and I am told that I do it well. I do my own laundry and handle all the household chores…with the exception of watering the plants, which Terri does.

When you enter our gate you will see that the new deck is a memorial to you. The plaque matches the one at Simpson University (which was placed at the base of the tree planted in your honor). To further celebrate and honor you, two scholarships were established in your name: one at Simpson for early childhood education and one at Westmont for a student who will become an elementary schoolteacher.

I have made some changes in the house and will make more. I gave the upstairs couch to Steen and Trina and the downstairs one to Todd. I now have a futon upstairs and a leather couch downstairs. In a few weeks, Jeannie Hilt, whose husband Steve died just two months after you, will help do some redecorating to make the house more masculine, while still honoring you. Your influence will always be there.

So, here I am on June 28, 2008, 50 years after I said, "I do." Bev, I am moving on and today is another big step in that direction. I will be writing to share what is happening personally as I move forward. But for today, the emphasis is on you and us.

I prayed this morning and thanked God for 50 years of relationship and more than 48 years of marriage. You were my anchor, my cheerleader, my confidant, my lover and the mother of my children. No matter where I go in the future, you will be there.

I had the main diamond in your wedding band removed and placed in my wedding band, which I wear on my right hand. It will be there until I die. I gave the other two diamonds to Terri and Trina. I have kept your ring and will give it to the children when I die so they will have a memory of our love and our marriage.

My life will definitely change as I move forward but you will always be part of it. In great measure, I am who I am because of you.

Happy Anniversary…I love you!

Letters to my children

June 27, 2008

Dear Terri,

Tomorrow is the 50th anniversary of my marriage to your mother. I am writing from the Fog Catcher Inn, where Mom and I spent many happy weekends. On one occasion our entire family was here. Do you remember?

I hope the album accompanying this note will serve as a reminder of – and tribute to – the woman who Bev Knowles Goehner was. I am so grateful for the 48-plus years we shared together, but sad we never got to celebrate this Golden moment together.

I am celebrating in my own way and I think your mom is celebrating too…in heaven. When I reach heaven maybe we can compare stories!

God blessed us with three wonderful children and you were our first. We often talked about the tough times, when you were young and we were involved in Youth for Christ. Your mom's partnership allowed me to experience years of ministry and her many sacrifices made possible many of the things we all enjoy today.

As you read through the album, I pray that it will bring back memories, as well as inspire you to strive to be the kind of woman your mom was. I trust you will love the Bible as she did, reading it for direction and God's will. May it give you hope and joy.

The recent months have been a difficult journey for you, too, Terri. You have walked a painful path and handled it with courage and faith. I think your mom knows what you're going through and is interceding on your behalf.

Thank you for living your faith before others. Like your mother, I am proud to call you my daughter.

Love, Dad

June 27, 2008

Dear Todd,

Tomorrow is the 50th anniversary of my marriage to your mother. I am writing from the Fog Catcher Inn, where Mom and I spent many happy weekends, and our family once enjoyed a brief vacation.

This is a bittersweet moment. Your mom and I had always looked forward to celebrating this Golden moment, but now we are apart. Somehow, I think she is celebrating in heaven as I am celebrating and remembering here. Maybe when I get to heaven we can compare notes!

God blessed us with three wonderful children. You were Mom's favorite son and my only son, for whom I had asked God since we got married. Your mom and I watched you as a child, and how you were often caught between your two sisters. Times were tough then, and all of you children remember "being poor." Todd, your mother's sacrifice made it all work; today, our family is enjoying the benefits of her commitment to us.

The enclosed is a small token of my love for you and my appreciation and love for your mother. It is impossible to love someone for nearly 50 years and not have your life profoundly influenced. One of those influences was her love for God and the Bible. I trust you will read one of her Bibles, treating it as the guide for your life and letting it give you hope and direction.

Todd, you are going through a difficult time in your life and you are handling it extremely well. I believe your mom is interceding on your behalf and she is so proud of you.

We all miss your mom, but I hope the enclosed will give you great memories and provide an example of how to live and how to die. Your mom did both extremely well.

Love, Dad

June 27, 2008

Dear Trina,

Tomorrow is the 50th anniversary of my marriage to your mother. I am writing from the Fog Catcher Inn, where Mom and I spent many happy weekends over the years. In fact, our entire family spent a long weekend here a few years ago.

June 28, 1958, was the happiest day of my life. I was marrying my high-school sweetheart and we were headed to Westmont College. Fifty years later, I have great memories and, although we are not sharing this Golden moment together, I am choosing to celebrate (and I believe she is celebrating in heaven). Maybe when I get there, we can compare notes!

God blessed us with three wonderful children and you were the youngest. Did you know your mom was disappointed when she found out she was pregnant with you? Once you arrived, however, she never stopped being thrilled about her "baby," the one who looked just like her.

Trina, as you grow older I see in you more and more of your mom. When I look at your picture, I see my wife in her 40s. I look at your mom's pictures and get a glimpse of what you will almost certainly look like in 20 years. What a gift!

The enclosed is a small token of my love for you and for your mom who influenced all of us in so many ways. Please enjoy the album, as both a memory and a memorial. Please accept this Bible as one of your mom's legacies: loving God and his Word.

Thank you for giving us three wonderful grandsons. They are such a joy and, as you know, your mom absolutely adored them. I think she's smiling in heaven right now, knowing that one of them is her in a male body!

Love, Dad

"It's been three years"

November 11, 2009

Dear Bev,
    It was three years ago yesterday that you went home to be with Jesus. At times yesterday it felt like it had been 10 years since you left; at other times, like 10 minutes.

    When I awoke yesterday I didn't know what to expect. Each year, on the anniversary of your death, I experience it differently. Two years ago, the entire family gathered in Santa Barbara to celebrate your life. At that time I gave special gifts to each child, grandchild, and Steen. Last year I worked the morning of Nov. 10, but took the afternoon off to remember you.

    This year I am in the midst of a nine-day trip to the East. As you predicted, I am doing a lot of traveling since I became a widower. Yesterday, I cleared my schedule (with the exception of one meeting) and spent the day reading, praying, working out and, then, socializing with friends. Last night I had dinner with Dave and Diane Buchanan, who have become dear friends. As you recall, we went to Radio City Hall in New York City with them one Christmas season.

    When I talked with Todd and Trina last night, we reviewed each of our days. Trina had a hard time, but Todd felt it was the best November 10th he has had in three years. I spoke with Terri briefly, but it was work-related.

    Your children are doing well.

    Todd has blossomed in his role at Project Understanding. He said that if you came back now, you might not recognize him! It would not be because of his physical appearance but because he is a changed man. Hon, he has grown so much since your death and has blossomed into a real leader in his organization. In fact, he is applying to become the next executive director, when the current director retires early next year. He and I spend many hours on the phone talking about non-profit organization management and he proudly calls me his coach.

Trina is working three-quarter time for one of David Odell's companies. (Yes, David Odell, who is now an entrepreneur and a wealthy businessman in Santa Barbara.) She is an active runner and the mother of your three teenage grandsons. Carter is now 13, Taylor 15 and Keaton turned 18 two days ago! As the years go by, she reminds me more and more of you. Always in motion, active with her boys, caring for friends and working to be a good wife. She is an amazing person and you would be so proud of her.

You would be thrilled at what fine young men your grandsons have become. You were a major influence in their early life and they have not forgotten you.

Keaton called me yesterday to see how I was doing and tell me how much he missed you. He is a senior at San Marcos, a body boarder (surfer) and works two jobs. He is applying for college and most likely will go to a school in San Diego (where the surfing is great!). He attended Urbana in December and I continue to pray that God will show Keaton clearly where he is to invest his life. As you know, we prayed from his childhood that God will call him into his harvest… wherever that might be. It appears that he will major in business and art. Several of his art pieces hang in my office – including one of you.

Taylor is 16 and beginning to drive. He is almost 6' tall, towering over me and his brothers. He has discovered a talent and passion for woodworking. He built his own shop in the garage and built a home-entertainment unit for my home and produces pens – ball points, roller balls and fountain pens. He even has his own business card! His other passions are volleyball (he received the Coaches Award during his freshman season) and the drums. Yes, he plays the drums!

Carter has developed into the dynamo we all thought he would be. Still short, he is an amazing young man. He taught himself the guitar and is now finishing his second CD. He can't sing (even though he tries), but he is a very good guitarist. No. 1 academically in his class and school, he is working toward attending Stanford on a golf scholarship! He began playing less than two years ago and is very good. He plays in lots of youth tournaments. Adults love him because of his keen mind and verbal skills. Oh yes, he still talks all the time!

Bev, Terri has had several challenges since you died. She tried hard to be my keeper and discovered that I needed to make it on my own. In February 2008, she was diagnosed with Stage-3 breast cancer. You were always afraid that her negligence to seek medical care would create a problem. She has gone through a number of treatments, including chemotherapy, radiation and a new drug, Herceptin. Unfortunately, the Herceptin damaged her heart and for the last eight months she has failed several heart tests, making it impossible to continue the treatment.

Last week she got good news. Her heart is back to normal and it has no doubt been aided by her new walking program, which was strongly encouraged by friends at the church. Terri is very active at SFC and serves in leadership. Our prayer is that she received enough help from the Herceptin that her cancer does not come back.

Your son-in-law, Steen, is doing well. He is a wonderful dad and is very successful as director of Elings Park in Santa Barbara. Did you know he started that job the week before you died? He also works part time for The Goehner Group, and has been a great support for me.

That brings me to my journey.

The past three years have been quite a pathway for me and, at times, very difficult. Sweetheart, I have survived and even thrived. I have grieved, celebrated our 50th wedding anniversary (alone) and redecorated our home to make it mine. Even though I have traveled a great deal, I have enjoyed my time at home.

The biggest news I have to share is that I am engaged to be married. As you know, we gave each other permission to remarry, should one of us die before the other. You know the person I am marrying and you will probably also remember that I said she was the one person I would never marry!

Caryl Taylor and I will be married on May 1, 2010. Our 30-year friendship grew into love and we have taken our time to build our relationship. I discovered that the Caryl who I thought was desperate to be married was instead a strong, courageous and caring woman who enjoyed her single life and had to process the entire idea of marriage.

This has been a very difficult decision, but I am convinced God has brought us together. Caryl has been very respectful of you and is not trying to replace you. As Carter says, "There is only one Nama!"

The family, with one exception, is thrilled. Unfortunately, Terri is having a very difficult time, and tension has resulted. My friends have encouraged me to move forward with our plans and we have.

We are selling both our homes and buying a new home in the San Jose area. It appears that I will need to work a few more years and she is willing to move south.

I have tears in my eyes as I conclude this letter. I am embarking on a new journey and this is my written goodbye to you. I must concentrate on my new marriage and give myself fully to my relationship with Caryl. However, as I said in my letter at your memorial service, I will always love you, my high-school sweetheart, and never forget you. I look forward to our reunion in heaven.

Love from your forever-grateful husband,

Don

Grief-recovery workshop presentation
  Saratoga Federated Church, April 26, 2009

The doctor said, "We did everything we could."

"Tell me straight: is she dead?"

Looking at me he said softly, "Yes."

And, so, my journey as a widower began.

During the past two and half years I have worked hard at grieving. There have been moments of intense pain and other times when I've realized that God has set me on a journey of growth. I want to share portions of that journey with you today.

I learned to lean into the pain

Kevin Friesen, music pastor at Saratoga Federated Church at that time, talked to me immediately after Bev's death, which happened suddenly in the late afternoon of November 10, 2006. He said, "I'm going to stay with you until Saturday night."

For 36 hours, Kevin was my constant companion. During that time he described three ways people react to pain. "Don," he lovingly challenged me, "You can deny it, but and it will ultimately catch up with you. You can try to avoid it and the result will be the same."

He suggested I lean into my pain, much like a skier leans downhill in order to keep moving – even though it can feel very risky. That's what I've chosen to do.

More opportunities to lean into the pain came quickly. Shortly after Bev's death I had to deal with an autopsy that revealed she had not had Alzheimer's (the diagnosis we received months before), but had died from a completely blocked carotid artery. I was devastated that day, learning she had suffered both a loss of memory and a misdiagnosis.

Within eight days of her death we held her memorial service (which she had planned meticulously and included my reading of a letter from me to her). It was painful to write (and read) and at times I had to stop and grieve, but it was a wonderful memorial service. It honored her, testified to her faith in Christ and helped people know the real Bev.

I continued to lean into pain the day after Thanksgiving, when I decorated for Christmas, as had been our custom for many years. As my daughter Terri and I put our decorations up we both grieved, realizing Bev would never spend another Christmas with us.

Two days after that first – and very hard – Christmas, we held her interment at the Monterey Cemetery. I remember how difficult it was to pick up the urn and place it in the niche. Really, the most difficult thing I have ever done. Keith, our pastor, asked "What will you miss most about her?" With tears in my eyes and a break in my voice, I said, "Her prayers."

Just six weeks after her death I discovered I was diabetic and began a whole new program of diet and exercise to control it. Bev had been the caregiver for my mother, so Terri and I now assumed that task. Difficult as it was, I began reading books on grief and revisited many of the same places where my wife and I loved to vacation. All of this in order to lean into the pain.

I learned you can choose your attitude

My good friend, Nancy Jensen, who had lost her husband several years before, said, "Don, you can't choose the circumstances but you can choose your attitude."

It was at that point in my journey I decided to choose an attitude of gratefulness, starting with gratitude for the 48 years of marriage we had had. I began to share my pain with others, instead of withdrawing and being maudlin. And, I sought to be closer to God, rather than to blame him.

Choosing the right attitude included being a role model for my children. For example, my son, Todd, was at a crossroad and I was fearful about how he would react to the loss of his mom. Would he return to behaviors that were not positive? To my delight and by the grace of God, he's become a brand-new man.

I learned to listen to good counsel

About four weeks after Bev died, a good friend, Tom Nelson, drove from Southern Calif. to San Jose to spend some time with me. He gave me three very strong pieces of advice, stressing that I needed to learn to:

- Do my own laundry
- Cook well enough to have guests over
- Live alone for at least three years and love it, avoiding the remarriage trap of so many widowers.

I took his advice and discovered a lot about who I really was – and was becoming. For years, I taught people that pain can produce growth. The question for me, now, was: Could I follow and live my own teaching?

I scheduled time for personal retreats and found people to help me

I began a new tradition of spending the first two to three days each year in a getaway retreat. The first was on Whidbey Island in Washington state, at the cottage owned by my cousin. I began my new life there on January 2, 2007. I spent the first 24 hours in silence and began to journal what I was feeling. I read to exhaustion because I wanted to learn from every book about grief and recovery I could get.

In addition to my reading and the retreats, I sought help from others who had walked a similar journey. I called widows and widowers and asked, "How did you do it?"

I also found someone to help me go Christmas shopping for my family. My need was real - I had never shopped for my daughters (that was always Bev's responsibility - and joy)! A longtime friend, Caryl Taylor, accompanied me (after being promised an In N Out burger if she would be my shopping consultant). It was a fun day, the family received far better gifts than they would have had I shopped alone, and I spent more money than I ever planned to spend.

I began to make adjustments

I began to realize I was single. I did not have a wife and for the first time in my entire adult life, I was not married. As Tom had suggested, I learned to cook (by inviting people to my home and to be my guinea pigs!). It wasn't too long before someone stopped me in church and asked me how they could get an invitation. I asked, "An invitation to what?"

"Dinner at your home. I hear you're an excellent cook."

I learned to do my laundry and because I'm so scrupulous, was able to master the task fairly quickly. In fact, my son told one of my daughters, "Dad was always more particular about his clothes and how they were hung and how his socks were placed in the drawers."

To my surprise, I discovered that coming home from business trips was easier than being on the road, contrary to what I had expected. On the road there was no one to call at night, which I did each night with Bev. Home felt safe.

One of the most difficult things was coming to church alone. Bev and I had always gone to church together and we'd served together. Here, at SFC, we'd worked in the hospitality ministry together.

It was odd, it was difficult and I developed a practice of coming late and leaving early to avoid as much conversation as possible. Frankly, I also didn't want women who were divorced or widowed seeking me out. I also discovered I was no longer invited to events Bev and I had attended as a couple.

Another adjustment came because we had been part of the Westmont trustees' family for many years. It felt odd to come to the meetings alone; Bev had always been a very central part of Trustee Weekends. (I found out after her death she was the "favorite spouse.") She welcomed the new spouses aboard, whether male or female, and ministered to the entire group in unique ways. Westmont trustee meetings were a time when I could share my grief journey. One year after her death, during our devotional time, I was allowed to talk about it very openly.

Finally, one of the major adjustments was changing bank accounts and updating records. That experience was ugly. I found banks, credit-card companies and department stores uncaring and difficult. But, adjustments are part of the journey and I continue to make them to this day.

I developed a new "normal"

Suddenly, I was spending my evenings alone. I'd always looked forward to time at home, being with Bev and talking with her about anything and everything. Now after work I was alone and sometimes in total silence (because I couldn't find any music that met my needs; I simply needed to work through my grief silently). With my diabetic condition as a motivator, I learned to cook healthy meals.

As I look back now I realize the changes in my cooking and eating were a gift from God. But more than anything, my new normal was that my wife was not coming back. I was Don Goehner and I was a widower. The first time I filled out a form as a widower I got tears in my eyes.

I learned to let others share my grief

This was risky. Would people get tired of me talking about my pain and changes? It turned out that talking about it openly made people more comfortable in discussing my situation with me. I began writing a journal and I added to it constantly for the first couple of years following her death.

A few friends had given me permission to call them on their cell phone if I felt lonely or needed some conversation, and I had done so on one or two occasions. Prior to Bev's death I had put together an e-mail list of folks who were praying for her recovery. After she died, I continued to report to this group for a year, updating them and letting them know how I was processing life as a widower.

In early 2007 I traveled to the Pacific Northwest and we held a memorial service in Bev's hometown of Wenatchee, Wash. I was amazed when I saw who was there. Two-thirds of the Apple Blossom Festival royalty from her senior year in high school were there and one of them told me, "Don, she became the woman we all wanted to be."

One of the most difficult times of sharing my grief was when I met with Ardelle Temanson, Bev's best friend since grade school. I flew to Minneapolis and spent two and a half days with Ardelle and her husband, Lee. We sat and cried together as we watched the DVD of Bev's memorial service.

I observed anniversaries and benchmarks

Following my wife's death on November 10, I marked the succeeding months - Dec. 10, Jan. 10, Feb. 10 and so forth - and took time every one of those days to deal with the pain. The first wedding anniversary following Bev's death - June 28, 2007 - was spent with my grandson, Keaton and friends David and Diane Buchanan in New York City. We went to the Statue of Liberty and the Empire State Building. I was so grateful to be active with people I loved, to be with my oldest grandson and to begin a new life, I didn't tell anyone it was my anniversary until we were driving back to New Jersey that evening.

For the first anniversary of Bev's death I went out of my way to make it a big deal. At the suggestion of a friend who had been recently widowed, I had special gifts made for each of my children, grandchildren, and my son-in-law. For our evening together I rented a stretch limo and a hotel suite in Santa Barbara.

After I picked up the family and we were driving to dinner, my son remarked, "We've done this before, Dad. We did this on you and Mom's 25th anniversary." I replied, "Todd, you're right. I wanted you all to remember how important your mom was and I thought this was one way of doing it."

We had a special dinner at the Harbor Restaurant and went back to my suite where we had the joy of sharing funny stories about Bev. Finally, I got to watch my family open their gifts and we took lots of photos.

I closed a 50-year chapter in my life

Bev and I had been married 48 years, but had been in a relationship for two years prior to that. So, during the two years following Bev's death, I went on vacations to places we had visited and loved. Once I took friends in North Carolina to a place Bev and I had especially enjoyed. Perhaps the toughest time was when I spent what would have been our 50th wedding anniversary at our favorite hotel on the Calif. coast and went to dinner at our favorite restaurant. There, in quietness and tears, I celebrated my 50th – and my wife!

What have I learned?
- You can't avoid pain; lean into it to bring about quicker, deeper healing.
- Grieving and healing is a long process. Arvin Engleson, a pastor at our church, says to plan on three to five years. When I first heard that, I thought he was wrong, but I believe he's right.
- Learn to live…and enjoy it. I like doing laundry; it allows me to multi-task. Cooking has become a hobby.
- Have a plan regarding your future, particularly regarding remarriage. (I set some criteria for any possible remarriage and I will stick to it.)
- Everyone grieves differently – me, my children and my friends.
- God is totally sufficient.

- I would not trade my growth over the last two and a half years for anything, although I wish I could have chosen another path.
- Scripture brings healing.
- Communion is different to me now, and so is prayer.
- I have no fear of death.
- I am a blessed man, seeking to be God's person.

My mom's graduation

February 25, 2007

At 7 a.m., the night RN at Fatima Villa, Mary Ellen, called to tell me Mom's death was imminent. After hearing that I didn't need to go immediately, I took time to shower and have breakfast. Little did I know that the next few hours would be a special gift for all of us!

I met Mary Ellen and she indicated that she thought Mom would be gone by noon. I had spoken with my sister, Eldora, and she had called my other sister, Elvera. My oldest daughter, Terri, had called my other children, Todd and Trina, to let them know about their grandmother's situation.

When I entered her room, it was clear she was in her final hours. At first I was confused and felt quite alone. It was one of those moments (and there have been many) when I really missed Bev, because it would have been so much easier with her at my side. I began to read Scripture to my mom and prayed silently that God would take her quickly.

A little after 9 a.m. the chaplain, Father Adel, came in and we talked. He had recently lost his mother and certainly understood my situation. As Father Adel and I prayed with Mom, his words were both eloquent and heartfelt (and sounded so much like an evangelical that I told some friends he prayed like a Baptist!).

He spoke to Mom, who by then was in a coma, and said, "Esther, this is Father Adel and your son, Don. We love you very much, but God loves you more. You have our permission to go be with God."

After the priest left, I went to my church and sought out my close friend and one of the pastors at my church, Kevin Friesen, and Terri. I asked Kevin if he could stop by my mom's room and asked both of them to update two of our other pastors, Arvin and Keith.

After picking up a hymnal, I headed back to Fatima Villa for an incredible two and a half hours with Mom. I sang her favorite hymns and gospel songs, and read Scriptures, including John 14:1-6 (one of many underlined in her Bible). I prayed aloud and silently.

Eldora and Elvera called, concerned that I was alone; frankly, I preferred it that way. In the midst of singing "Amazing Grace," Arvin walked in and joined me on the last two verses. He knelt by Mom's bed, placed his hand on her arm and prayed, committing her to the Lord and asking that her spirit would soon join God's spirit.

About 30 minutes later, Kevin arrived and, shortly thereafter, Terri. The four of us gathered around the bed and prayed for Mom and for the family. Keith called to say he was delayed, so Terri and I went to lunch.

We saw our friends, the McAfees, at the restaurant and Marguerite told me the music-ministry staff had prayed for Mom and our family. Eric invited us to call if we wanted someone to stop by and sit with us during the afternoon.

Just as we were finishing lunch, the nurse called to say Mom had stopped breathing and we should return. As we headed back, I called Eldora and Keith, and Terri called Todd and Trina.

We hurried into Fatima Villa and ran upstairs to her room. To our amazement, I was told she had started to breathe again. Only my mom could pull off something like that!

For the next 20 minutes we watched as Mom's breathing slowed down. Her favorite nurse's aide, Ada, sat by the bed holding her hand. At last she stopped breathing and the nurse checked for pulse and blood pressure. Nothing…Mom had gone home to be with her Lord, her husband, Bev and her family forever. Praise God!

Messages from our prayer team

I was repeatedly and deeply blessed by the many e-mails I received following Bev's death, including these.

> Don, I am a man of words, but they seem entirely inadequate now. Just know that we love you, and that I continue to pray for you on a daily basis.
>
> You and Bev remain a part of our lives, even if separated by distance or time and space. Grateful for your friendship. And, grateful for your ministry and your witness in this moment. Not what you wanted, but what you have been given. And, what you have stewarded well. Bless you my friend,
>
> Stan

―⚘―

> My, how our hearts ache for you and your family at this difficult time. Thank you so very much for sharing your thoughts with us. You have been in our prayers for some time now and we will continue to pray for you, your family and for those who are still very much going through the grieving process.
>
> Your sharing is so helpful to those of us who care so much for Bev and you, but who could not be at the service. You have filled in some of the blanks, my friend, and for that we are grateful.

Following Bev's death, I tried on so many occasions to pick up the phone and call you. But for some reason, I could not bring myself to push the "Talk" button. Perhaps it was just that I could not bear to hear the voice of a deeply grieved Don Goehner. Or, perhaps it was God's way of telling me, "Not now; Don needs some time with his own thoughts." Whatever, your note now opens the door for me. We'll talk soon. Always know that we, with our God, love you very much.

Ed

—⋙—

May the Lord encourage you with His Word today:

Praise be to the God and Father of our Lord Jesus Christ! In his great mercy he has given us new birth into a living hope through the resurrection of Jesus Christ from the dead, and into an inheritance that can never perish, spoil or fade - kept in heaven for you, who through faith are shielded by God's power until the coming of the salvation that is ready to be revealed in the last time. In this you greatly rejoice, though now for a little while you may have had to suffer grief in all kinds of trials. These have come so that your faith - of greater worth than gold, which perishes even though refined by fire - may be proved genuine and may result in praise, glory and honor when Jesus Christ is revealed. Though you have not seen him, you love him; and even though you do not see him now, you believe in him and are filled with an inexpressible and glorious joy, for you are receiving the goal of your faith, the salvation of your souls.   1 Peter 1:3-9

Love in Christ,

Dan and Lynn

—⁂—

Thank you so much for the e-mail and thank you for sharing your heart so transparently. I pray for all of you every day; it is so helpful to know how you would like those prayers directed. It is also a great encouragement to see all the things God is doing in the lives of others as a result of Bev's death. She had such an impact for the kingdom of God in life – it is only fitting that her impact continues after her death as well. God has been faithful – He has promised and we do not labor in vain.

We will continue to pray for you as you return to work. I'm sure it will be with a much different energy, but I also know that God will sustain you as He has given you such a great business. We will continue to pray for Terri, Todd, Steen and Trina. They will have to take their own journey in their own way, but we will uphold them in prayer as they find their way through.

Finally, thank you so much for the wonderful service that you and Terri held for Bev. As difficult as it was, it was such a fitting tribute to her and I know that you guys worked so diligently to give Bev the day she deserved. She would have been so proud! We value all of you more than we can express. Love,

Brenda

Please know that you and your family remain in our prayers and that God is blessing so many as you share this painful journey. The specific request for your neighborhood and doctor are most compelling. "The fragrance of Christ in this neighborhood" is the earthly version of what Jesus said to Bev with open arms, "Well done my good and faithful servant." What tears of joy this brings and, no doubt, what a huge hole it leaves behind.

You are a good man, a faithful example of one who has poured (and continues to pour) his life into others, who bathes his soul in the soothing grace of God's Word...and it exudes from your being as you share the journey. May God bless it, multiply its impact and expand His Kingdom as eternity is made drastically different for those who watch, see Jesus in you and your family... and then choose to believe!! If I were a preacher I'd say, "AMEN!!"

From the outside in, these last several weeks have placed a wonderful exclamation point on Bev's life here on earth, and a ringing endorsement of her "graduation."

Know that you are loved and prayed for, daily. In His matchless Grace,

Gordon

> First of all, Courtney and I want to send our deepest respects to you and your family after hearing news of the passing of Bev. We are so sad to see such a good and godly person as Bev leave us all so soon and so suddenly. We are comforted knowing that Bev is in a better place now. She is looking down at all she knows, with that smiling face we grew to know and love as we passed her on the way to our condo near yours.
>
> When I think of Bev I recall this passage, "Do not forget to entertain strangers, for by so doing some people have entertained angels without knowing it." Hebrews 13:12
>
> You and Bev were two of the first to greet us when we moved in – thank you for your kindness and friendliness! Your neighbor and friends,
>
> Dan and Courtney

Messages to our prayer team

I sent many e-mails to our prayer team (which grew to include dozens of friends, family members, ministry associates and business colleagues and clients) over the course of this journey – Bev's illness and death, as well as my steps toward healing. Excerpts from a few of the e-mails are included here, to help underscore what a huge support and blessing these partners-in-grief were for me.

From: Don Goehner

Sent: Wednesday, November 08, 2006 10:29 PM

Subject: Bev's update

Good evening,

Some of you are getting this type of e-mail for the first time, but I know you are people of prayer and we need a prayer team.

As most of you know, Bev was discovered by a stranger in a parking lot and the stranger reached Terri at our office and called 911. The EMTs treated it as a potential stroke and had Bev transported to best hospital in this area for treating strokes. The Body of Christ jumped into action and Terri was strongly supported while I traveled home.

This morning, when Terri and I walked in, Bev was awake and recognized us. They took out the breathing tube in the late morning and she was able to eat lunch. She was transferred to a regular room at 6 p.m.

Here is what we know, what we don't know, our praises to God and our prayer requests:

1. Bev did not have a stroke but, rather, a seizure.

2. The stranger saw Bev sitting in her car when she entered the laundromat across the parking lot from the restaurant which Bev was attempting to enter. When the woman exited approximately 20 minutes later, she felt God directing to check on

the lady who was still sitting in the car. Arriving, she instantly knew Bev was in trouble and called for help.

3. There is a five-centimeter cyst on Bev's brain which may have contributed to the seizure. At first we were told that it was the cause, but now we don't know.

4. This incident is probably not linked to her MCI condition, which is now being referred to by the medical staff as pre-Alzheimer's.

5. They have ruled out surgery and are giving her medication to prevent seizures.

6. Her right hand and arm are not responding as yet and there is some limited use.

7. She is going to receive occupational and physical therapy.

8. We still have as many questions as answers.

Praises:

1. Thankfully, Bev was not driving at the time of the seizure; if she had, the seizure could have been life-threatening.

2. God's hand was evident in the "angel" who showed up.

3. They were able to reach me in time so I could get home the same evening.

4. Our children have arrived and been a real source of strength.

5. Our church family has been terrific, as has our pastoral staff.

6. We know people across the country are praying and we feel it.

7. The Goehner Group team has rallied to take my assignments so I can spend my time with Bev without any worries about business responsibilities.

Our prayer requests:

1. That we would receive a clearer definition of the cause of the seizure (while realizing we may never have that privilege).

2. That Bev would regain full use of her right hand.

3. That Bev would overcome the confusion she experienced this afternoon and early evening.

We are standing on the promises of God's Word, resting in his grace and experiencing the sense of God's people praying. Thank you. We stand humbled and grateful before you.

Don

From: Don Goehner

Sent: Thursday, November 09, 2006 5:39 AM

Subject: Bev's illness and Journey

I am writing to ask for your prayers.

Bev was hospitalized following a seizure on Tuesday afternoon in the parking lot of a KFC a few blocks from our office. I will forward an e-mail to our prayer list that outlines what happened and our prayer requests.

I had intended to bring you and others up to date on Bev's physical and mental journey this week before this incident happened.

For the past several months she has been tested for memory issues and we just received the final diagnosis: mild cognitive impairment. In 50 percent of the cases, the person becomes an Alzheimer's patient. Bev appears to be in that category.

After much prayer, we decided to go public with the information in order to have as many people praying as possible. She is receiving the latest drugs and we are asking people to pray that God would intervene and slow down the disease and, if he chooses, heal her.

We also discovered she has an enlarged heart and her lung capacity is not at 100 percent. For years she has suffered with back pain and that has flared up during this time at well. She is a patient at Stanford Neurology and she is working with a sports-medicine doctor for her back issues. We are scheduled to see a cardiologist regarding her heart in 10 days.

So, this latest development is extremely troubling. I will add you to our prayer-chain list and make certain you get all the updates.

We are resting on God's Word, his grace and, in the midst of stormy waters, we are experiencing his peace.

Don

—⚌—

From: Don Goehner

Sent: Friday, November 10, 2006 9:06 AM

Subject: Friday update

Good morning,

Thanks for all your prayers and support. This will be a short update because we are preparing for Bev to return home late this afternoon or possibly tomorrow morning.

We praise God for her rather quick recovery from the seizure, but there are still concerns. Our prayer requests:

1. That she would regain full use of her right hand and arm. The doctors are not certain what caused the trauma but we all believe that she never left

the car and she had a violent episode in which she kept hitting the steering wheel with her face and arms. Her eyeglasses frames were bent and broken, and she had a cut in her eyebrow that required stitches. Bev told us her whole body was shaking and she kept hitting things.

2. That the doctors would find the cause of the seizure. They are now of the opinion that the cyst on her brain was not the cause.

3. That we can find home-care assistance. The person who worked for my mom and we love dearly is not available.

4. That the neurologist and neurosurgeon will have wisdom as they decide what to do about the cyst. It is the size of an orange and filled with liquid. They are inclined to leave it alone because it has not grown and is most certainly benign. It is not causing the brain to swell and they indicate that draining it is a very delicate procedure that they prefer to do only as a last resort. They will monitor it carefully. (Here is a praise: the Stanford neurologist working with Bev on her MCI condition is a partner with the neurosurgeon).

5. That she will not lose her driving privileges (a real possibility).

Finally, pray for Terri, Todd and Trina. They have become painfully aware that their mother has a serious condition and it appears that it is progressing.

On this Veterans Day I am aware of those who made the ultimate sacrifice for the freedom we enjoy and grateful for a country with such wonderful medical care. Also, a country where we can worship freely and where, as a result, God's people care for each other. Thank you all for the notes, e-mails, calls -- and most of all -- the prayers. You will never know how much they have lifted us up.

We love you all,

Don

From: Don Goehner

Sent: Friday, November 10, 2006 4:59 PM

Subject: Bev is with Jesus

This is the hardest message I have ever had to write.

This afternoon, at approximately 2:35, Bev collapsed just after she finished her walk with a physical therapist that was prepping her to go home. I had been on the phone when Todd's girlfriend found me. I rushed to the room to see the nurses frantically working on Bev. We were asked to leave and for 45 minutes they worked desperately to save her. Because they do not know what happened, an autopsy will be conducted because it was such a shock to the medical staff.

I am surrounded by friends and my family from

Southern Calif. is en route. I asked God last night for his will to be done because it was becoming evident that Bev was in the initial stages of Alzheimer's. I pleaded for a few more years, but also said that if she had the disease, to take her quickly. He answered my prayer and she will never become someone who is looked at strangely or seems to be odd. She is with Jesus, her parents and my dad. Praise God.

Just one more word: The service will be next Saturday, November 18 at 11 a.m., at Saratoga Federated Church, 20390 Park Place, Saratoga, CA 95070.

Thanks for being our prayer partners on this journey...it just ended sooner than I thought. You are so special to me and our family.

Don

From: Don Goehner

Sent: Thursday, November 30, 2006 5:41 AM

Subject: An update on the "new" journey

Dear special friends,

On the eve of the 21st day since I sent what I described as "the hardest e-mail I have ever written," I have chosen to give you an update on my new journey...one which I did not choose, but one which I am working hard to embrace...filled with emotion, gratefulness, amazement at God's grace, and the incredible realization that God uses people like you to be the hands and feet of Jesus to me and my family.

I will keep this as short as possible and I may stop once or twice because my eyes well up with tears, but I am finding that grieving is not only private but, to some degree, public, as I allow the community of God to minister to me.

I have three reactions: Gratefulness in the midst of pain, praise for God's hand and the continued need for prayer (not just for me, but the many hurting people around me who are walking in their own grief and loss).

Gratefulness:

• For a wonderful memorial service, attended by more than 500 people who, by their presence, honored Bev, me, and my family.

• For a number of non-churched neighbors who attended the service and with whom I have shared my faith. I am planning a Christmas open house to continue the opportunity for friendship and attempt to be a small reminder of Bev.

• The several friends and pastoral staff who have been available 24/7 for phone calls and conversations, including prayer over the phone.

• Our senior pastor and his family, who gave Terri and me the gift of a Thanksgiving afternoon and evening as their only guests, and loved us unconditionally.

• An associate pastor who spent the first 36 hours after Bev's death with me.

- The more-than 100 e-mails; dozens of phone messages; nearly 200 cards (more are still arriving), flowers, and food; and families that opened their homes for my family after the service.

- The widows and widowers who have contacted me and are open to dialog and interaction, because they know what I feel; many are several years ahead of me in the grieving and recovery process.

- My children, son-in-law, girlfriend of my son and three wonderful grandsons...all of whom loved Ben and grieve with me...each in their own way.

- A sense that this tragedy is helping to bring my children closer together, knowing Bev's death isn't a tragedy, but an evidence of God's mercy (although, for those of us who remain, it's terribly painful).

- For a God who has been ever-present when I have cried out for relief of the pain, as well as helping me get through the loneliness. I told my doctor that if my Christian faith didn't work in this circumstance, that so-called faith was not genuine. I have had one conversation with him about my faith and we are planning to have lunch together. Please pray for Ed DeWees. He is a wonderful man who has been a rock throughout this ordeal, and our relationship is more than doctor-patient. He has reached out to Terri and me in incredible ways.

- For a church that has loved me and Terri in unbelievable ways, from the 10 people who showed up at the hospital 10 minutes after Bev's graduation, to the service, to the continual care and prayer.

• For my Goehner Group team, who have taken over projects, allowing me to have a time of grief before heading back to work.

• Friends from Simpson University who drove down to visit Bev, only to arrive just after she died. They stayed to comfort us and have been a source of support ever since.

• My administrative assistant, Linda Connors, who has been an anchor of strength for me.

Praise for God's hand:

• The passerby who was, indeed, an angel in disguise, who came to Bev's aid and gave our family and me three days with Bev. (We continue to be in contact because this woman feels she did not do enough for Bev. I plan to meet with her next week and, hopefully, minister to her. During our last phone conversation she could hardly speak.)

• That my cell phone was turned on in Spokane (rare, during interviews) so I could call to get help for Terri and make plans to get home the same night.

• That Trina and Todd were able to come from Southern Calif. and have a last day with their mom.

• That a friend who had stents the week following Bev's service was on the same hospital floor as Bev. God gave me the confidence to visit him and the nurses who served Bev…it was a healing process.

- For the opportunities I've had to share my faith during this process, including a letter to each of her doctors thanking them for their care; expressing my confidence that she is with God; and our confidence we will see her again. That communication has led to at least three conversations and the promise of continued dialogue regarding her progression into Alzheimer's, and the implications of that for my children.

- A friend who was available to talk with I received the autopsy report and was feeling deeply the finality of Bev's death.

- Much more.

Continued need for prayer:

- My family as we grieve in our own ways. Some have chosen grief counseling and others have not. Simply pray that each will grieve and God will provide the healing.

- My grandsons, who are also processing this. Pray that I will be a grandfather to whom they can share their feelings of all sorts. I can't be their Nama, but I want to be someone who continues investing in their lives.

- Me, as I return to work this weekend. I confessed to a friend this week that I found myself not caring about my business/ministry...I know that seems impossible.

- Opportunities where I can share my faith.

- Our family as we prepare for Bev's internment.

- Further definition from the autopsy report. (Bev

died of a "massive blood clot" that went to both lungs. In the words of the attending physician, "She never had a chance." We are puzzled, because they can find no reason for the clot and she had no history of clots. We also have no answers as to why she had the seizure.)

• Todd, Terri and Trina, as I work with the doctors to see if blood clots are a family medical issue that could affect them.

• Me, that I will, on a daily basis, deal with the reality of being a widower and the loss and awkwardness that comes with that new role.

I'm sorry…I said I wouldn't be long, but my heart is full and you have been such an incredible part of the journey!

Gratefully,

Don

—⁂—

From: Don Goehner

Sent: Friday, November 09, 2007 11:47 AM

Subject: It's been a year!

Dear special people,

November 9 and 10 will always be incredibly significant for me:

November 9, 1998 – We buried my father.

November 9, 2005 – My friend, Roger Post, graduated to heaven.

November 9, 1991 – My first grandson, Keaton, was born.

November 10, 2006 – Bev graduated.

Today is Keaton's 16th birthday and I remember his comment to me this summer when we traveled to the East Coast together. "Grampa, I'm glad Nama didn't die on my birthday." I am also glad, but I am sorry that Bev is missing this milestone in his life.

Terri and I will be leaving in a few hours for Santa Barbara where our entire family will gather tomorrow night for dinner and a time to remember Bev. Your prayers will be appreciated. I will give you a brief update next week as we close one chapter and open another. The year of firsts is over, but we all feel the holidays may be more difficult; we were in shock last year.

Just yesterday I realized that the clothes I was wearing had been purchased after Bev's death last November. If she saw me today she would say things like:

"What's with the haircut?"

"What is the thing in the den/office?" (Just my new futon.)

"You've got a leather couch, just like a man!"

"Don, you did a good job on the new deck."

And finally, "Give everybody a hug and tell them I love them."

I have dreamt about Bev twice: Dream No. 1 – She returned and I wanted to tell everyone. But she simply said, "I want you to know I am OK." Dream No. 2 – Last night she and I were hurrying to get somewhere…then I woke up.

God has been ever-present and God's people (like you) have held up my arms and lifted my spirit. Thank you for your ministry to me and my family.

Rejoicing in the midst of pain,

Don Goehner

From: Don Goehner

Sent: Wednesday, November 21, 2007 3:45 PM

Subject: The end and a new beginning

Dear prayer team and family,

On Sunday, the 18th, we reached the first anniversary of Bev's memorial service. Tomorrow we will observe our second Thanksgiving without her. Given that I was in Nepal for Thanksgiving 2005, it will have been three years since we shared this special day.

This is my last update to all of you, written with the following thoughts in mind:

• My gratefulness for your support and prayer during the past year.

- My appreciation for all the notes, calls and e-mails I have received.
- My gratefulness to God for his faithfulness and grace.

What have I learned in the past 12 months?
- God is sovereign.
- God is sufficient.
- God is faithful.
- Prayer is powerful.
- Pain gives us options. Retreat from it or seek to confront it and grow through it.
- God's people are remarkable and they want to reach out.
- My family is a gift from God and they are all the products of Bev's incredible life and love.
- Bev raised me. The man I am today is, in large part, due to her love, patience, and faithfulness.
- The entire Don Goehner family is a reflection of her faith and lifestyle.
- We all grieve differently.
- If you loved deeply, you will grieve deeply.
- Life goes on and it is important to not get stuck.

Many of you have asked about our family's weekend in Santa Barbara together. Thanks for praying. Your prayers were answered. From the stretch limo to dinner at the Harbor Restaurant, to our time together in my hotel, I felt God's presence. We laughed and we shared. I had the privilege of giving gifts to the family in memory of Bev, gifts that I trust will be keepsakes and provide great memories of this remarkable woman of God.

How can you pray for me and the family now? That God will continue his healing in each of our lives and that we will look back on this past year as a time of spiritual growth.

In closing, I want to leave you with a passage of Scripture I found on March 1, just days after my mom died.

"But he knows the way that I take; when he has tested me, I will come forth as gold. My feet have closely followed his steps; I have kept to his way without turning aside. I have not departed from the commands of his lips; I have treasured the words of his mouth more than my daily bread." Job 23:10-12

I have experienced Verse 10 and I am seeking to experience Verses 11-12.

Happy Thanksgiving and THANK YOU FOR YOUR LOVE AND YOUR PRAYERS!!

Don Goehner

From: Don Goehner
Sent: Monday, March 16, 2009 5:34 PM
Subject: One-year update on Terri

Dear Prayer Team,

Several have asked for an update on Terri and I have been remiss in getting the information to all of you who have so faithfully prayed for her.

She was diagnosed on February 28 of last year, and I still remember hearing the dreaded words: breast cancer. Her first chemo appointment was March 13, 2008. Since that time she has had eight chemo treatments, 28 radiation treatments and nine Herceptin treatments. As you know, we received the great news on December 16 that she was cancer-free. Since then, she has continued the Herceptin treatments. On February 13, we met with Dr. Vempaty, the oncologist and learned:

• The cancer isn't showing up on the PET scan. At this point, they've found no active cancer cells.

• The Herceptin treatments have lowered the possibility of reoccurrence from 70-80 percent to 30-40 percent. We like that reduction in odds!

• I asked about the possibility of any permanent heart damage from the Herceptin. The doctor's response was that only 1-2 percent have permanent heart damage, but the heart must be monitored on a regular basis. If it drops below 50, treatment will stop to allow the heart to heal.

Earlier, I wrote about Terri's heart test today

and asked for prayer. The doctor just called and indicated that Terri's score had dropped to 35 and the Herceptin treatments will be stopped for six weeks. She receives a new medication tomorrow which she will take for six weeks. At that point they will retest and, hopefully, the treatment can begin again.

Terri has a very good attitude but, frankly, Dad is a little discouraged. She has been so brave and tough, and was pleased that she was halfway through the Herceptin treatment that would have finished in August. Now we don't know.

However, in the big picture, we have made so much progress and have much for which to give thanks to God. It is amazing that she is cancer-free! I want to keep that perspective and consider this as a bump in the road. So, here are our prayer requests:

• That Terri will not suffer the possible side effects (swollen tongue, dry cough and lowered blood pressure) from the new drug.

• That the drug will strengthen the heart so she can begin treatments again in six weeks.

• That Terri will keep her eye on the final goal of completing the Herceptin treatment.

• That her dad will keep his eye on the final goal as well.

Let me balance the prayer requests with some wonderful praises:

• Praise for a cancer-free condition (after being at Stage 3 and almost Stage 4).

- The reoccurrence rate has been cut in half.
- That Terri has handled the treatment as well as she has.
- Terri has missed very few days of work.
- She directed her fourth women's retreat for our church, with a record number attending.
- We are blessed to have over 75 people praying on a regular basis.
- God has been so good!

Thanks for all you have done. Thanks for caring and praying.

A grateful dad,

Don Goehner

Books on grieving

When God Interrupts: Finding new Life Through Unwanted Change
    M. Craig Barnes, Intervarsity Press, 1996

Praying through the Tough Times
    Lloyd John Ogilvie, Harvest House, 2005

Living with Mystery: Finding God in the Midst of Unanswered Questions
    Stacey Padrick, Bethany House, 2001

A Grace Disguised, How the Soul Grows Through Loss (Expanded Edition),
    Jerry Sittser, Zondervan 2005

www.ingramcontent.com/pod-product-compliance
Lightning Source LLC
LaVergne TN
LVHW051554070426
835507LV00021B/2571